contents

D1515398

Key

- Number and Place value
- Addition and Subtraction
- Multiplication and Division
- Shape, Data, Probability and Measure
- Fractions and Decimals
- Algebra
- Mixed Operations

How to use this book

Read the instructions carefully before each set of questions.

The first page of each section will have a title telling you what the next few pages are about.

Your teacher may tell you to GRAB something that might help you answer the questions.

Sometimes a character will give you a tip.

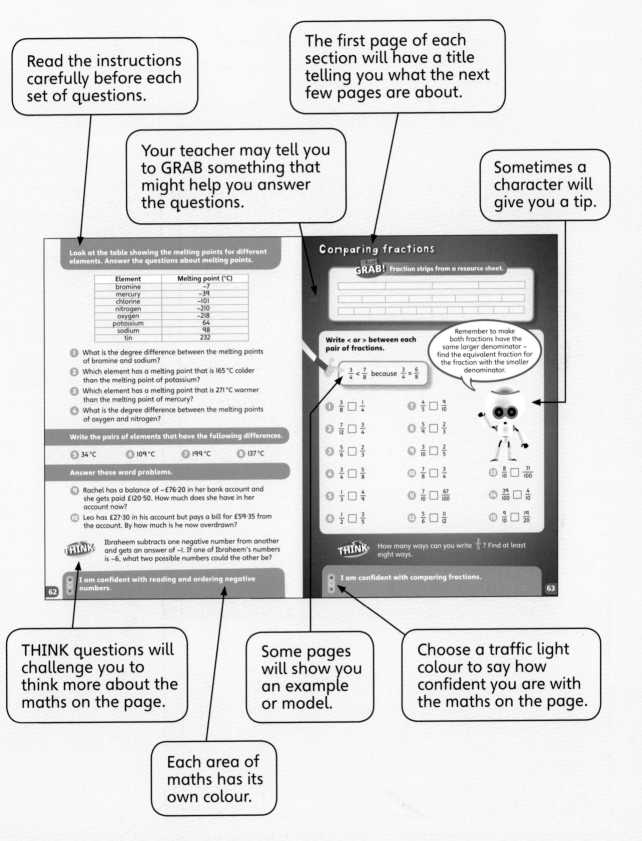

Look at the table showing the melting points for different elements. Answer the questions about melting points.

Element	Melting point (°C)
bromine	−7
mercury	−39
chlorine	−101
nitrogen	−210
oxygen	−218
potassium	64
sodium	98
tin	232

1. What is the degree difference between the melting points of bromine and sodium?
2. Which element has a melting point that is 165 °C colder than the melting point of potassium?
3. Which element has a melting point that is 271 °C warmer than the melting point of mercury?
4. What is the degree difference between the melting points of oxygen and nitrogen?

Write the pairs of elements that have the following differences.

5. 34 °C   6. 109 °C   7. 199 °C   8. 137 °C

Answer these word problems.

9. Rachel has a balance of −£76·20 in her bank account and she gets paid £120·50. How much does she have in her account now?
10. Leo has £27·30 in his account but pays a bill for £59·35 from the account. By how much is he now overdrawn?

THINK Ibraheem subtracts one negative number from another and gets an answer of −1. If one of Ibraheem's numbers is −6, what two possible numbers could the other be?

I am confident with reading and ordering negative numbers.

62

Comparing fractions

GRAB! Fraction strips from a resource sheet.

Write < or > between each pair of fractions.

$\frac{3}{4} < \frac{7}{8}$ because $\frac{3}{4} = \frac{6}{8}$

Remember to make both fractions have the same larger denominator – find the equivalent fraction for the fraction with the smaller denominator.

1. $\frac{3}{8} \square \frac{1}{4}$ 7. $\frac{4}{5} \square \frac{9}{10}$

2. $\frac{7}{12} \square \frac{3}{4}$ 8. $\frac{5}{9} \square \frac{2}{3}$

3. $\frac{5}{6} \square \frac{2}{3}$ 9. $\frac{3}{10} \square \frac{2}{5}$

4. $\frac{3}{4} \square \frac{5}{8}$ 10. $\frac{7}{8} \square \frac{3}{4}$ 13. $\frac{8}{10} \square \frac{71}{100}$

5. $\frac{1}{3} \square \frac{4}{9}$ 11. $\frac{7}{10} \square \frac{67}{100}$ 14. $\frac{39}{100} \square \frac{4}{10}$

6. $\frac{1}{2} \square \frac{3}{5}$ 12. $\frac{5}{6} \square \frac{11}{12}$ 15. $\frac{9}{10} \square \frac{19}{20}$

THINK How many ways can you write $\frac{2}{5}$? Find at least eight ways.

I am confident with comparing fractions.

63

THINK questions will challenge you to think more about the maths on the page.

Some pages will show you an example or model.

Choose a traffic light colour to say how confident you are with the maths on the page.

Each area of maths has its own colour.

6-digit numbers

Write these numbers in figures and then put them in order from smallest to largest.

1 Two hundred and fifty-three thousand, four hundred and nineteen

2 Nine hundred and four thousand, five hundred and sixty-eight

3 Seven hundred and forty-eight thousand, three hundred and fifteen

Copy these pairs of numbers and write < or > between them.

4 253 670   261 984

5 427 094   416 940

6 716 205   617 205

7 606 899   607 007

8 911 919   919 199

9 787 878   787 787

Complete these subtractions.

10 985 613 − ☐ = 905 613

11 410 763 − ☐ = 410 063

12 826 495 − ☐ = 26 495

13 745 522 − ☐ = 740 522

14 601 304 − ☐ = 1304

15 520 482 − ☐ = 520 402

THINK Using the digits 1–6, write a number as close as possible to 500 000.

○ **I am confident with reading and writing 6-digit numbers.**

4

Write these numbers in figures. Then put the < or > sign between them.

1. Five hundred and sixty-two thousand, and forty-five
   Five hundred and three thousand, four hundred and fifty-two

   [_____]   [_____]

Write < or > between these numbers.
Write two numbers that come between each pair.

2. 452 604   425 640

3. 301 234   310 432

4. 824 215   824 511

5. 703 462   730 462

Complete these subtractions.

6. 555 555 – [ ] = 505 550

7. 555 555 – [ ] = 550 055

8. 555 555 – [ ] = 505 050

9. 555 555 – [ ] = 550 505

 Using two different digits (neither is 5!) and four zeros, what is the closest number you can make to 555 555?

I am confident with reading and writing 6-digit numbers.

5

1-place, 2-place and 3-place decimals

Work out the answers to the calculations. Use the place-value grid to help you.

 $3 \cdot 17 \times 10 = 31 \cdot 7$

$48\,506 \div 100 = 485 \cdot 06$

	10 000s	1000s	100s	10s	1s	•	0·1s	0·01s
× 10					3	•	1	7
				3	1	•	7	
÷ 100	4	8	5	0	6			
				4	8	5	• 0	6

① 6345 ÷ 10 = ☐

6345 ÷ 100 = ☐

6345 ÷ 1000 = ☐

② 73 652 ÷ 10 = ☐

73 652 ÷ 100 = ☐

73 652 ÷ 1000 = ☐

③ 30 060 ÷ 10 = ☐

30 060 ÷ 100 = ☐

30 060 ÷ 1000 = ☐

④ 36·24 × 10 = ☐

36·24 × 100 = ☐

36·24 × 1000 = ☐

⑤ 188·4 × 10 = ☐

188·4 × 100 = ☐

188·4 × 1000 = ☐

⑥ 1·572 × 10 = ☐

1·572 × 100 = ☐

1·572 × 1000 = ☐

 **THINK** A number is divided by 100. The answer is 0·03. What was the number?

I am confident with reading 1-place and 2-place decimals and multiplying and dividing by 10, 100 and 1000.

Work out the answers to the calculations. Use the place-value grid to help you.

① 43·06 × [ ] = 4306

② 7242·1 × [ ] = 724210

③ 846250 ÷ [ ] = 8462·5

④ 34·62 × [ ] = 34620

⑤ 78846 ÷ [ ] = 788·46

⑥ 354·13 × [ ] = 3541·3

⑦ 71700 ÷ [ ] = 71·7

⑧ 64·6 × [ ] = 64600

⑨ 5390 ÷ [ ] = 5·39

⑩ 400·06 × [ ] = 40006

 Paige thinks of a whole number less than 2000. When this number is divided by 100 the answer ends in the digits 0·6. What is the number Paige is thinking of?

I am confident with reading 1-place and 2-place decimals and multiplying and dividing by 10, 100 and 1000.

Write < or > between the numbers.

1 5·624   5·523

2 4·174   4·721

3 6·143   6·056

4 0·468   0·621

Write all six numbers from the grid below in order, from the smallest to the largest.

5

	1s	•	$\frac{1}{10s}$ 0·1s	$\frac{1}{100s}$ 0·01s	$\frac{1}{1000s}$ 0·001s
a	4	•	2	5	3
b	5	•	3	4	2
c	4	•	5	2	3
d	4	•	3	5	2
e	5	•	4	2	3
f	5	•	3	2	4

Use the digits 1–4 to write three numbers between 2 and 3 that are 3-place decimals. Write them in order from the smallest to the largest.

I am confident with reading and ordering 1-, 2- and 3-place decimals.

Write which number each arrow is pointing at. Then write it rounded to the nearest whole number.

a = 0·2 0

1 b = ☐ ☐

2 c = ☐ ☐

3 d = ☐ ☐

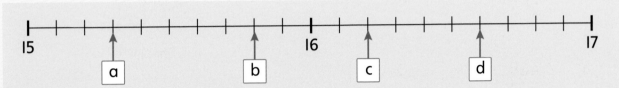

4 a = ☐ ☐

5 b = ☐ ☐

6 c = ☐ ☐

7 d = ☐ ☐

Write which number each arrow is pointing at. Then write it rounded to the nearest tenth.

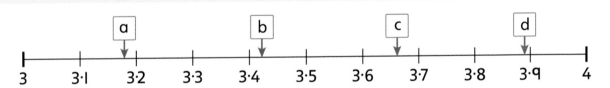

a = 3·18 3·2

8 b = ☐ ☐

9 c = ☐ ☐

10 d = ☐ ☐

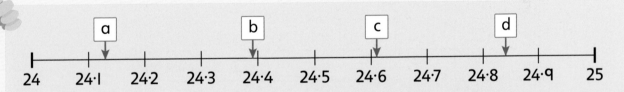

11 a = ☐ ☐

12 b = ☐ ☐

13 c = ☐ ☐

14 d = ☐ ☐

Write three decimal numbers. Each must have two decimal places that round to 0·5 as their nearest tenth. One must have 1 as one of its digits.

I am confident with reading and rounding 1-, 2- and 3-place decimals.

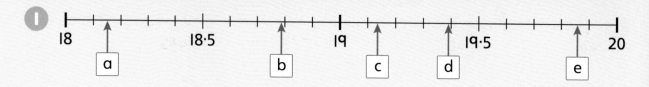

1

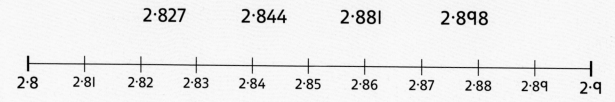

	Number	Rounded to nearest tenth	Rounded to nearest whole number
a			
b			
c			
d			
e			

2 Copy this number line and mark on these four numbers:

2·827   2·844   2·881   2·898

2·8   2·81   2·82   2·83   2·84   2·85   2·86   2·87   2·88   2·89   2·9

3 Draw a line from 4·8 to 5·1 with all the hundredths marked. Write on:

4·917   4·884   5·026   5·057

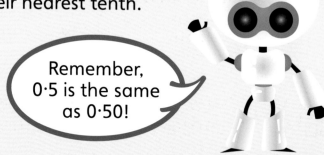

THINK Write three decimal numbers that each have three decimal places. They should round to 0·5 as their nearest tenth.

Remember, 0·5 is the same as 0·50!

1

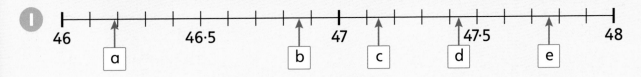

	Number	Rounded to nearest tenth	Rounded to nearest whole number
a			
b			
c			
d			
e			

2 Copy and complete this table and correct any mistakes..

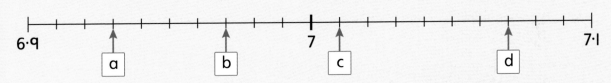

	Number	Rounded to nearest tenth	Rounded to nearest whole number
a			7
b		7	
c	7·01		
d			7·1

3 Draw a line from 11·8 to 12·1 with all the hundredths marked.
Write on:

      11·811   12·079   11·856   11·933

 THINK How many decimal numbers with three decimal places are there that round to 0·55 as their nearest hundredth?

I am confident with reading 1-, 2- and 3-place decimals.

Converting fractions and decimals

Write the equivalent fraction or decimal for each question.

1 $\frac{1}{10} = \square$

2 $0 \cdot 6 = \square$

3 $\frac{7}{10} = \square$

4 $0 \cdot 9 = \square$

5 $\frac{27}{100} = \square$

6 $0 \cdot 31 = \square$

7 $\frac{63}{100} = \square$

8 $0 \cdot 19 = \square$

9 $\frac{1}{4} = \square$

10 $0 \cdot 01 = \square$

11 $\frac{3}{100} = \square$

12 $0 \cdot 07 = \square$

Copy and complete these questions.

13 $0 \cdot 75 = \frac{\square}{100} = \frac{3}{\square}$

14 $0 \cdot 05 = \frac{\square}{100} = \frac{1}{\square}$

15 $0 \cdot 24 = \frac{\square}{100} = \frac{6}{\square}$

16 $0 \cdot 96 = \frac{\square}{100} = \frac{\square}{25}$

THINK Write a 2-place decimal number which is less than 1 and has one zero after the decimal point. Then write it as a fraction.

I am confident with converting between fractions and decimals.

Write the equivalent fraction or decimal for each question.

1 $\frac{53}{100}$ = ☐

2 0·75 = ☐

3 0·23 = ☐

4 $\frac{91}{100}$ = ☐

5 0·7 = ☐

6 $\frac{1}{4}$ = ☐

7 $\frac{3}{10}$ = ☐

8 0·09 = ☐

Write the equivalent fraction or decimal for each question.

9 $\frac{456}{1000}$ = ☐

10 0·801 = ☐

11 $\frac{195}{1000}$ = ☐

12 0·327 = ☐

13 0·363 = ☐

14 $\frac{125}{1000}$ = ☐

15 $\frac{43}{1000}$ = ☐

16 0·009 = ☐

 Write a 3-place decimal number which is less than 1 and has two zeros after the decimal point. Then write it as a fraction.

I am confident with converting between fractions and decimals.

13

Addition of whole numbers

Answer these additions using mental strategies.

1. $302\,041 + 80\,000 = \square$

2. $162\,395 + 300\,200 = \square$

3. $972\,816 + 3023 = \square$

4. $375\,562 + 20\,030 = \square$

5. $634\,436 + 2002 = \square$

6. $743\,061 + 106\,000 = \square$

7. $382 + 499 = \square$

8. $7095 + 801 = \square$

9. $463 + 399 = \square$

10. $4184 + 601 = \square$

11. $3072 + 702 = \square$

12. $4173 + 798 = \square$

13. $76 + 59 = \square$

14. $82 + 63 = \square$

15. $326 + 84 = \square$

16. $657 + 65 = \square$

17. $37 + 52 + 48 = \square$

18. $81 + 76 + 23 = \square$

19. $80 + 30 + 60 + 90 = \square$

20. $700 + 500 + 600 = \square$

21. $15\,000 + 43\,000 = \square$

22. $9000 + 3000 + 2000 + 8000 = \square$

 **THINK** What clues do numbers give you to show they can be added in your head?

I am confident with solving additions with mental strategies.

Answer these additions using mental strategies.

1 $102\,041 + 80\,204 = \square$

2 $6085 + 903 = \square$

3 $70 + 40 + 50 + 90 = \square$

4 $406\,301 + 310\,400 = \square$

5 $836 + 84 = \square$

6 $1276 + 699 = \square$

7 $77 + 69 = \square$

8 $686\,784 + 3006 = \square$

9 $700 + 900 + 800 = \square$

10 $3766 + 59 = \square$

11 $382 + 697 = \square$

12 $305\,562 + 20\,099 = \square$

13 $13\,072 + 906 = \square$

14 $85\,000 + 42\,000 = \square$

15 $84 + 73 + 63 = \square$

16 $634\,436 + 102\,142 = \square$

17 $7268 + 598 = \square$

18 $47 + 71 + 59 = \square$

19 $683\,069 + 104\,300 = \square$

20 $5000 + 13\,000 + 7000 = \square$

21 $847 + 74 = \square$

22 $4604 + 603 = \square$

 THINK   Add three numbers to get 100. No two digits in the question should be the same.

Answer these additions using the column method.

6829 + 3134 + 5406 =

```
  6000 + 800 + 20 + 9
  3000 + 100 + 30 + 4
+ 5000 + 400 +  0 + 6
 ─────────────────────
 14000  1300   50  19  = 15369
```

```
    6 8 2 9
    3 1 3 4
+   5 4 0 6
      1
  1 5 3 6 9
```

1 37 254 + 14 432 = ☐

2 93 104 + 15 237 = ☐

3 36 435 + 31 829 = ☐

4 56 752 + 13 189 = ☐

5 85 662 + 17 635 = ☐

Answer these additions using the column method.

6 6254 + 5162 + 5481 = ☐

7 3285 + 1068 + 1476 = ☐

8 3894 + 7542 + 4782 = ☐

9 5828 + 4932 + 3932 = ☐

10 8279 + 4478 + 6157 = ☐

 If we add 6666 to 7777 do we get a number with lots of digits the same? Try it to see if your guess is right!

I am confident with solving additions using the column method.

31797 + 82562 =

30 000 + 1000 + 300 + 90 + 7
+ 80 000 + 2000 + 500 + 60 + 2
―――――――――――――――――――――――
110 000   3000   800   150   9 = 113959

```
  3 1 3 9 7
+ 8 2 5 6 2
      ₁
―――――――――
1 1 3 9 5 9
```

THINK How can you tell where a carry will be needed?
Spot two questions where a 100 000 will be made.

1   46 563
    + 26 574
    ―――――――

2   43 728
    + 38 462
    ―――――――

3   56 846
    + 39 385
    ―――――――

4   63 742
    + 17 469
    ―――――――

5   72 843
    + 63 979
    ―――――――

6   81 778
    + 38 751
    ―――――――

7   59 815
    + 44 189
    ―――――――

8   82 363
    + 56 638
    ―――――――

9   75 435
          7543
    +   9246
    ―――――――

10   11 062
          9437
    +   9384
    ―――――――

11   23 686
          7735
    +   6680
    ―――――――

12   98 547
          9785
    +   4859
    ―――――――

I am confident with solving additions using the column
method.

Addition of decimals and whole numbers

Complete these additions. Use the inverse operation to help you.

1 $32 + \boxed{} = 100$

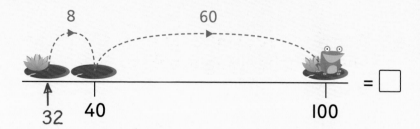

$= \boxed{}$

2 $69 + \boxed{} = 100$

4 $56 + \boxed{} = 100$

3 $\boxed{} + 23 = 100$

5 $\boxed{} + 39 = 100$

Complete these decimal additions.

$3·69 + 0·31 = 4$

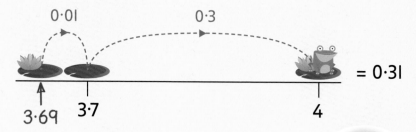

$= 0·31$

6 $8·42 + \boxed{} = 9$

9 $6·29 + \boxed{} = 7$

7 $5·81 + \boxed{} = 6$

10 $4·14 + \boxed{} = 5$

8 $3·37 + \boxed{} = 4$

11 $7·76 + \boxed{} = 8$

THINK Two 1-place decimal numbers add to make 2. If none of the digits in the two numbers are the same, what could the numbers be?

⦿ **I am confident with solving decimal additions using**
○ **mental strategies.**

1. Calculate the perimeter of a triangle with sides of 2·3 cm, 1·5 cm and 3·7 cm.

2. A fork-lift truck picks up two crates. One weighs 4·63 kg and the other weighs 4·99 kg. What is the total mass of the two crates?

3. Look at this table of surfing scores. Add the scores and see which surfer won.

	Surf 1	Surf 2	Total
Surfer 1	8·04	6·1	
Surfer 2	6·47	3·02	
Surfer 3	7·21	8·51	
Surfer 4	3·99	4·76	
Surfer 5	5·6	6·07	

 Two 2-place decimal numbers add to make 2. If none of the digits in the two numbers are the same, what could the numbers be?

I am confident with solving decimal additions using mental strategies.

Use column addition to solve these additions.

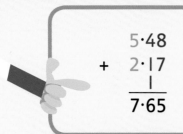

$$
\begin{array}{r}
5 \cdot 48 \\
+ \quad 2 \cdot 17 \\
\underline{1 \qquad} \\
7 \cdot 65
\end{array}
$$

Answer these additions.

1 $\begin{array}{r} 3 \cdot 52 \\ + \ 9 \cdot 16 \\ \hline \end{array}$ **3** $\begin{array}{r} 4 \cdot 27 \\ + \ 1 \cdot 36 \\ \hline \end{array}$ **5** $\begin{array}{r} 6 \cdot 33 \\ + \ 7 \cdot 45 \\ \hline \end{array}$ **7** $\begin{array}{r} 7 \cdot 26 \\ + \ 8 \cdot 91 \\ \hline \end{array}$

2 $\begin{array}{r} 8 \cdot 73 \\ + \ 1 \cdot 41 \\ \hline \end{array}$ **4** $\begin{array}{r} 3 \cdot 62 \\ + \ 4 \cdot 84 \\ \hline \end{array}$ **6** $\begin{array}{r} 5 \cdot 68 \\ + \ 5 \cdot 15 \\ \hline \end{array}$ **8** $\begin{array}{r} 3 \cdot 68 \\ + \ 2 \cdot 94 \\ \hline \end{array}$

Look at the items. Find the total cost for each question.

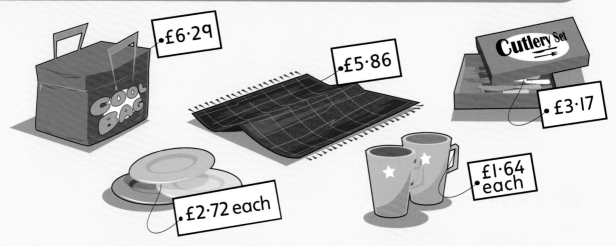

•£6·29

•£5·86

Cutlery Set

•£3·17

£1·64 each

•£2·72 each

9 a cool bag and cutlery set   **11** a mug and a cool bag

10 a rug and one plate   **12** two mugs

 Write two numbers that add to make £20 where the pence end in 3 and 7.

○
○ **I am confident with solving decimal additions using**
○ **the column method.**

Answer these additions.

1.
```
   3·25
   1·19
+  2·43
_____
```

2.
```
   7·61
   1·92
+  1·35
_____
```

3.
```
   5·26
   4·07
+  4·63
_____
```

4.
```
   8·63
   6·85
+  4·71
_____
```

5.
```
   4·78
   2·47
+  1·79
_____
```

6.
```
   6·76
   7·89
+  6·82
_____
```

Look at the items. Find the total cost for each question.

£3·17

£7·68

£6·29

£5·86

£1·64 each

£2·72 each

7. a football and shorts

8. a skipping rope and tennis racket

9. a rugby ball and shorts

10. a skipping rope, a flying disc and shorts

 THINK Write two numbers that add to make £20 where no digit number is the same in either of the two numbers.

○
○ **I am confident with solving decimal additions using**
○ **the column method.**

21

Add these decimals mentally.

Is it easy-peasy place value or are you adding the decimals like you would add 2-digit numbers?

1 3·5 + 2·7 = ☐

4 5·22 + 1·45 = ☐

2 10·24 + 4·1 = ☐

5 5·71 + 8·83 = ☐

3 5·32 + 1·84 = ☐

6 8·52 + 9·4 = ☐

Solve these additions using a written method.

7
```
  25·48
+ 16·91
------
```

9
```
  53·31
+ 27·59
------
```

Write these out vertically!

8
```
  29·13
+ 17·68
------
```

10
```
  49·38
+ 32·07
------
```

 Two amounts of money add to give £10.
One is less than £5 and one is more.
In both, the pence are multiples of 4p.
What could the two amounts be?

○
○ **I am confident with solving decimal additions using**
○ **mental and column methods.**

Solve these additions using mental and column methods.

1 3·71 + 8·29 = ☐

4 54·2 + 6·9 = ☐

2 14·05
   + 7·3
   ——————

5 12·99 + 5·4 = ☐

3 63·77
   + 24·86
   ——————

6 34·71
   + 18·47
   ——————

Solve these additions. Decide which method to use for each question.

7 3·69 + 6·2 = ☐

10 58·25 + 19·78 = ☐

8 66·3 + 24·85 = ☐

11 22·6 + 31·16 = ☐

9 3·99 + 7·3 = ☐

12 7·45 + 6·55 = ☐

A mystery number is added to a near multiple of £20 to give £46·64. Give two suggestions as to what the mystery number could be.

I am confident with solving decimal additions using the mental and column methods.

Solve these additions using mental and column methods.

1 23·81 + 4·65 = ☐

2 19·07 + 3·2 = ☐

3 47·85 + 95 = ☐

4 16·8 + 2·99 = ☐

5 48·44 + 3·87 = ☐

6 5·04 + 0·73 = ☐

7 73·36 + 1·64 = ☐

8 4·82 + 1·28 = ☐

9 13·99 + 2·7 = ☐

10 63·72 + 4·57 = ☐

11 53·01 + 5·81 = ☐

12 77·74 + 6·69 = ☐

**THINK** Two amounts of money add to give £45. In one amount, the number of pounds is the number of pounds in the other amount reversed. In both amounts, the pence are multiples of 4p. What could the amounts be?

I am confident with solving decimal additions using the mental and column methods.

Missing number problems

Find the missing value for each calculation.

1. $a + 64 = 92$

2. $42 - b = 39$

3. $6\frac{1}{2} - c = 5$

4. $64 \div d = 16$

5. $1\frac{1}{2} \times e = 6$

6. $3 \times f + 1 = 31$

7. $45 \times g = 180$

8. $2 \times h = 25 + h$

9. $i \div 8 = 12$

10. $100 - j = j - 40$

Find out what number each letter represents.

 THINK

$2 \times b + a = 14$

$2 \times a + b = 13$

Find out what a and b are.

○
○   **I am confident with solving missing number problems.**
○

25

Find the missing value for each calculation.

1. $20 - a = 17$ $a = \square$

2. $3 \times b = 15$ $b = \square$

3. $y - 10 = 25$ $y = \square$

4. $x + 6 = 14$ $x = \square$

5. $4 \times c + 1 = 41$ $c = \square$

6. $25 \div a = 5$ $a = \square$

7. $x + 20 = 36$ $x = \square$

8. $7 \times c = 21$ $c = \square$

9. $9 + b + 2 = 20$ $b = \square$

10. $20 - y = 5$ $y = \square$

Remember, each letter is just a missing number!

Write pairs of numbers which could make each calculation work.

11. $45 + a + b = 55$

12. $13 - c - d = 6$

13. $m + 7 + n = 15$

14. $3 \times g \times h = 30$

 Write your own equation with an unknown value in it. Work out the answer and test it on a partner.

I am confident with solving missing number problems.

$a + 45 + b = 54$

$b - a = 3$

> $a + b$ must equal 9. Looking at the second equation, $b - a$ must equal 3. So b must be 6 and a must be 3.

Think about what the numbers could be for the first equation in each pair. Use the clues in the second equation to find what the numbers are.

1. $c + 25 + d = 35$ $c - d = 2$ $c = \square$ $d = \square$

2. $a \times b \times 2 = 24$ $a - b = 1$ $a = \square$ $b = \square$

3. $34 - x - y = 27$ $x - y = 5$ $x = \square$ $y = \square$

4. $45 + g + h = 57$ $g \times h = 11$ $g = \square$ $h = \square$

5. $c \times d \times 3 = 60$ $d - c = 8$ $c = \square$ $d = \square$

6. $11 - m - n = 6$ $m \times n = 6$ $m = \square$ $n = \square$

7. $36 \div x = 3y$ $x + y = 8$ $x = \square$ $y = \square$

 If $c + d + 5 = c \times d$ what could the numbers be?

I am confident with solving missing number problems.

Finding missing angles and lengths

Find the value of each letter.

1

$x° \quad 60°$

$x = \boxed{}$

2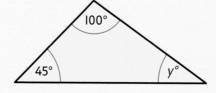

$100°$

$45° \quad y°$

$y = \boxed{}$

3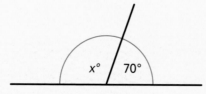

$x° \quad 70°$

$x = \boxed{}$

4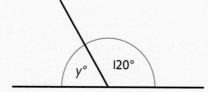

$y° \quad 120°$

$y = \boxed{}$

5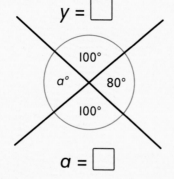

$100°$

$a° \quad 80°$

$100°$

$a = \boxed{}$

6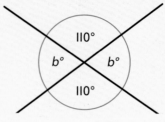

$110°$

$b° \quad b°$

$110°$

$b = \boxed{}$

7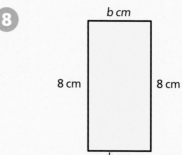

$c°$

$75° \quad 75°$

$c°$

$c = \boxed{}$

8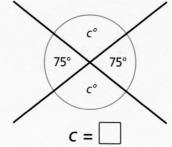

b cm

8 cm   8 cm

b cm

perimeter = 24 cm

$b = \boxed{}$

9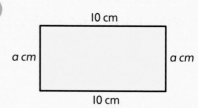

10 cm

a cm   a cm

10 cm

perimeter = 30 cm

$a = \boxed{}$

using brackets

When there are no brackets, always work out the multiplication or division first.

Work out each set of calculations.

1 $5 \times 12 - 8 = \square$

$(5 \times 12) - 8 = \square$

$5 \times (12 - 8) = \square$

2 $10 \div 2 + 3 = \square$

$(10 \div 2) + 3 = \square$

$10 \div (2 + 3) = \square$

3 $4 + 8 \times 6 = \square$

$(4 + 8) \times 6 = \square$

$4 + (8 \times 6) = \square$

4 $20 - 8 \div 2 = \square$

$(20 - 8) \div 2 = \square$

$20 - (8 \div 2) = \square$

5 Write a number sentence laid out like this:

$$a \diamondsuit b \diamondsuit c = \square$$

where a, b and c are whole numbers and one of them is a 2-digit number. One of the diamonds is either × or ÷ and the other diamond is either + or −.

Add brackets to your calculations, putting them around one of the parts of the calculation. E.g. $5 \times (7 + 4)$.

Work out this calculation, remembering that we do the brackets first. Record the answer.

Move the brackets to the other part of the calculation and record the answer. E.g. $(5 \times 7) + 4$.

Compare all three answers. What do you notice? Repeat.

THINK Work out $2 \times (5 + 3)$ and then work out $(2 \times 5) + (2 \times 3)$. What do you notice? Is the same true if you change the 5s and 3s for different numbers?

I am confident with using brackets in mixed calculations.

29

1. $(2 + 5) \times 3 = \square$ $2 + (5 \times 3) = \square$

2. $(42 - 5) \times 7 = \square$ $42 - (5 \times 7) = \square$

3. $(12 \div 6) - 2 = \square$ $12 \div (6 - 2) = \square$

> Think carefully about the order of the operations

4. $4 + 5 \times 3 = \square$ $(4 + 5) \times 3 = \square$

5. $10 + 6 \div 2 = \square$ $10 + (6 \div 2) = \square$

6. $(3 + \frac{1}{2}) \times 2 = \square$ $3 + (\frac{1}{2} \times 2) = \square$

7. $4 \times 6 - 2 = \square$ $4 \times (6 - 2) = \square$

8. $24 - (4 \times 3) = \square$ $(24 - 4) \times 3 = \square$

9. $5 - 1\frac{1}{2} \times 2 = \square$ $(5 - 1\frac{1}{2}) \times 2 = \square$

10. $(3 \times 2) + (6 \div 2) = \square$ $3 \times (2 + 6) \div 2 = \square$

 THINK Write your own pair of calculations with the same number and signs, but with the brackets in different places so that you get two different answers.

● ○ ○ **I am confident with calculations involving brackets, and the order of operations.**

Solve these calculations.

1 $6 + 2 \times 4 = \square$

2 $(3 + 9) \div 3 = \square$

3 $10 - 3 \times 2 = \square$

4 $(9 - 3) \times 2 = \square$

5 $7 \times 3 + 2 = \square$

6 $(12 - 10) \div 2 = \square$

7 $80 \div 10 - 6 = \square$

8 $33 \div (4 + 7) = \square$

9 $(24 + 4) \div 4 = \square$

10 $12 \div 2 + 4 \times 3 = \square$

11 $12 \div (2 + 4) \times 3 = \square$

12 $(14 - 7) \times 7 + 4 = \square$

Solve these word problems.

13 Lucy is 80 cm shorter than her Dad. Her younger brother, Ben, is half the height of Lucy. If their Dad is 190 cm tall, how tall is Ben?

14 Katie has two cats, Poppy and Treacle. Poppy eats $4\frac{1}{2}$ pouches of cat food a day and Treacle eats $6\frac{1}{2}$ pouches a day. Katie wants to buy enough pouches for two weeks. How many pouches must she buy?

15 Andy has 42 football cards and Kevin has 38. Their friend, Rachel, has three times as many cards as Andy and Kevin have altogether. How many cards does Rachel have?

16 Rani runs twice a week. Each week she does a short run that is 7 km and a long run that is 14 km. How far does she run in four weeks?

THINK How many calculations with different answers can you write using the numbers 12, 4 and 5 once each and the operations × and +? You may use brackets as well.

Write the weight of each book in grams.

2·03 kg = 2030 g

3
4·05 kg

6
4·27 kg

1
3·104 kg

4
6·009 kg

7
0·12 kg

2
1·002 kg

5
0·85 kg

8
1·77 kg

Copy and complete these conversions.

9   45 kg = ☐ tonnes

13   530 g = ☐ kg

10   56 kg = ☐ tonnes

14   7367 g = ☐ kg

11   4·6 tonnes = ☐ kg

15   54 600 kg = ☐ tonnes

12   100 g = ☐ kg

16   10 tonnes = ☐ g

 Weigh a book. Approximately how many books weigh 1 tonne? Discuss with your partner.

I am confident with converting between grams and kilograms.

Converting lengths

Write the length of each monster in centimetres and millimetres.

0·36 m = 36 cm
= 360 mm

3

0·74 m

6

0·66 m

1

0·48 m

4

1·26 m

7

1·07 m

2

0·66 m

5

1·33 m

8

1·04 m

How many reels of cable are needed to make 1 km of cable?

100 m

10

50 m

12

250 m

14

500 m

10 × 100 m = 1 km, so 10 reels of cable

9

200 m

11

125 m

13

25 m

15

62·5 m

16 How many reels are needed to lay 14 m of electrical cable?

 THINK Measure your partner's height in metres. Repeat, changing roles. How many of you, when placed end to end, make 1 km?

○
○ **I am confident with converting lengths.**
○

Finding time intervals

Copy and complete this table to show how long each mountain biker took in a time trial.

	Start time	End time	Time taken	Position
Rory	14:48	15:16	28 minutes	
Sharon	14:54	15:32		
Eliza	15:38	16:05		
Dev	15:49	17:04		
Harrison	16:29	17:18		
Priya	16:36	18:11		
Precious	16:44	17:39		
Jack	17:37	18:18		

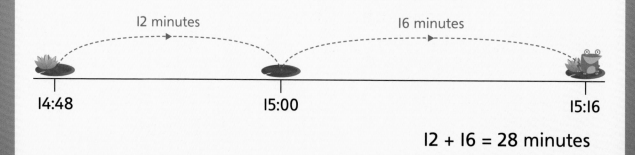

12 minutes   16 minutes

14:48   15:00   15:16

12 + 16 = 28 minutes

THINK Dave started 2 minutes after Alice. Alice started at 12:45 and finished at 13:12. She was 4 minutes slower than Dave. What time did Dave start and finish?

I am confident with finding time intervals.

Copy and complete this table to show how long each runner took in a time trial.

	Start time	End time	Time taken	Position
Allie	09:48	12:13		
Tom	09:32	13:07		
Dave	09:41	13:27		
Shifa	09:52	14:48		
Alfie	10:41	13:36		
Nelson	10:26	14:19		
Adaya	10:35	14:17		
Emile	10:49	13:22		

Use Frog to help work out the time each runner took.

THINK Two runners started at the same time. One was 30 minutes faster than the other. One ended the race at 15:45. What are the possible start and end times for these two runners?

I am confident with finding time intervals.

Copy and complete this table. Fill in the missing times and positions for each walker in a time trial.

	Start time	End time	Time taken	Position
Sam	11:44	15:38		
Oliver	10:38	14:53		
Isla	10:57		4 hours 12 minutes	
Craig	11:39		3 hours 42 minutes	
Millan		16:29	2 hours 16 minutes	
Daniel	11:17	16:28		
Tami		17:16	3 hours 38 minutes	
Keira		17:04	4 hours 9 minutes	

 A music track lasts for 8 minutes 47·8 seconds. If the track is played on the radio, starting at 55 minutes and 12 seconds past 3, what time did the track finish?

I am confident with finding time intervals.

Subtraction strategies

Start with the number given below. Then use the numbers on the balloons to create and solve three subtractions for each question.

1 5826

2 2870

3 6917

4 7091

 13

 2532

 699

5 Which method did you use for the pink balloon?

6 Which method did you use for the blue balloon?

7 Which method did you use for the yellow balloon?

8 Check your answers for questions 1 to 4 using addition.

THINK How many subtractions can Frog do where the larger number is 1004 and the first hop is 24?

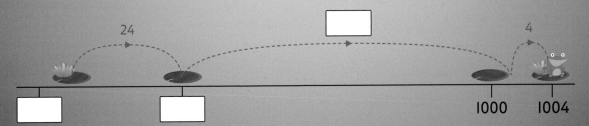

24   4

1000   1004

○ **I am confident with using mental strategies to complete**
○○ **subtractions.**
○○

Choose how to solve each of these subtractions.

1.
$$56\,473 - 4\,392$$

2.
$$85\,645 - 8\,923$$

3.
$$27\,744 - 5\,239$$

4.
$$19\,513 - 8\,846$$

5.
$$84\,372 - 63\,191$$

6.
$$96\,940 - 75\,319$$

7.
$$40\,463 - 39\,271$$

8.
$$27\,328 - 15\,029$$

9.
$$72\,244 - 35\,735$$

10.
$$50\,020 - 19\,509$$

11.
$$556\,324 - 413\,362$$

12.
$$573\,500 - 491\,356$$

Remember, you can use Frog if you need to.

Check two subtractions using column additions. Choose the two which will be easiest to check. Give reasons why these are the easiest to check!

I am confident with subtracting 5- and 6-digit numbers.

Solve each subtraction.

1
```
  65 042
−   4 327
```

2
```
  57 135
−   3 493
```

3
```
  23 055
−   2 289
```

4
```
  79 588
− 28 846
```

5
```
  67 014
− 53 198
```

6
```
  72 743
− 65 339
```

7
```
  78 078
− 32 279
```

8
```
  21 712
− 15 029
```

9
```
  82 041
− 37 889
```

10
```
  525 020
− 121 509
```

11
```
  516 803
− 408 589
```

12
```
  620 086
− 411 391
```

 Choose the three hardest subtractions on the page and check your answers in three different ways: (i) using addition, (ii) subtracting the answer from the larger number, (iii) using Frog to do the subtraction. Why were the ones you chose the hardest?

I am confident with subtracting 5- and 6-digit numbers.

Decimal subtractions

Answer these subtractions using place value.

1. $8{\cdot}3 - 4{\cdot}1 = \boxed{}$

3. $6{\cdot}42 - 1{\cdot}01 = \boxed{}$

2. $14{\cdot}8 - 3{\cdot}2 = \boxed{}$

4. $26{\cdot}38 - 10{\cdot}2 = \boxed{}$

Answer these subtractions using Frog.

$7{\cdot}3 - 6{\cdot}7 = \boxed{}$

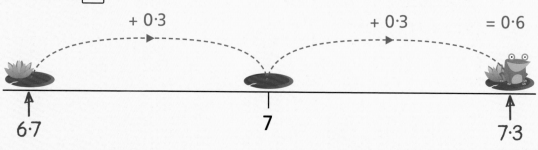

+ 0·3   + 0·3   = 0·6

6·7   7   7·3

5. $8{\cdot}4 - 7{\cdot}7 = \boxed{}$

7. $6{\cdot}2 - 3{\cdot}9 = \boxed{}$

6. $14{\cdot}3 - 11{\cdot}8 = \boxed{}$

8. $11{\cdot}1 - 6{\cdot}3 = \boxed{}$

Answer these decimal subtractions using rounding.

$8{\cdot}3 - 1{\cdot}99 = \boxed{}$

$8{\cdot}3 - 2 = 6{\cdot}3$ $6{\cdot}3 + 0{\cdot}01 = 6{\cdot}31$

> Round the number being subtracted to make these easier to answer mentally.

9. $4{\cdot}6 - 1{\cdot}99 = \boxed{}$

11. $6{\cdot}25 - 3{\cdot}99 = \boxed{}$

10. $7{\cdot}3 - 2{\cdot}01 = \boxed{}$

12. $20{\cdot}6 - 11{\cdot}01 = \boxed{}$

THINK Write a rule to explain how to solve $4{\cdot}5 - 1{\cdot}9$.

I am confident with using mental strategies to complete subtractions.

Choose how to answer these decimal subtractions.

1 13·36 – 5·99 = ☐

2 41·37 – 20·04 = ☐

3 3·82 – 0·3 = ☐

4 12·3 – 9·7 = ☐

5 54·72 – 8·99 = ☐

6 3·4 – 2·8 = ☐

7 18·27 – 3·99 = ☐

8 14·89 – 1·03 = ☐

9 13·2 – 9·6 = ☐

10 58·39 – 16·04 = ☐

11 40·13 – 7·99 = ☐

12 22·3 – 18·8 = ☐

13 11·27 – 4·99 = ☐

14 85·66 – 30·3 = ☐

15 64·4 – 58·8 = ☐

Look at each question. Is it a 'no work', Frog or rounding question?

 Which subtraction did you find easiest and why? Write one of each type of subtraction with a clue as to how to solve it.

I am confident with using mental strategies to complete subtractions.

43

4·24 − 3·78 = 0·46

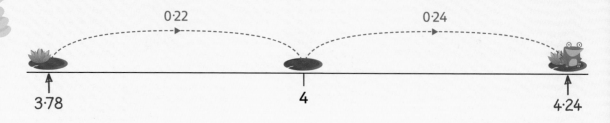

0·22   0·24

3·78   4   4·24

① 2·37 − 1·82 = ☐

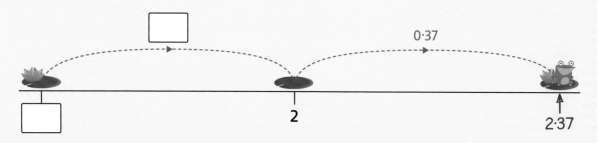

0·37

2   2·37

② 6·14 − 5·67 = ☐

③ 3·2 − 1·78 = ☐

④ 8·21 − 7·69 = ☐

⑤ 7·09 − 6·73 = ☐

⑥ 4·1 − 3·65 = ☐

⑦ 5·3 − 4·72 = ☐

⑧ 9·17 − 8·81 = ☐

⑨ 6·04 − 5·66 = ☐

⑩ 10·26 − 9·83 = ☐

THINK

Start with 5·5 and subtract 1·78. How many times will you be able to do this?

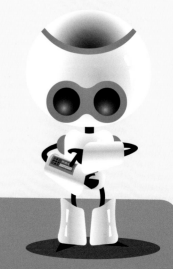

I am confident with using Frog to complete subtractions.

44

Answer these decimal subtractions using Frog.

1 8·7 – 7·63 = ☐

2 7·2 – 6·78 = ☐

3 8·4 – 6·29 = ☐

4 5·9 – 3·63 = ☐

5 6·4 – 3·96 = ☐

6 5·3 – 4·72 = ☐

7 9·1 – 5·09 = ☐

8 6·4 – 5·27 = ☐

9 8·5 – 3·66 = ☐

10 6·7 – 2·66 = ☐

Answer these decimal subtractions.

11 6·44 – 2·93 = ☐

12 9·25 – 2·84 = ☐

13 7·33 – 5·76 = ☐

14 8·27 – 2·67 = ☐

15 11·54 – 2·86 = ☐

16 12·36 – 10·74 = ☐

 1·78 is subtracted from two numbers. The answer of the first subtraction is 0·1 more than the answer of the second subtraction. The answer is between 0·5 and 1. What could both subtractions be?

1 £20 − £17·48 = ☐

£2

£18

£20

2 £50 − £34·28 = ☐

4 £100 − £85·93 = ☐

3 £100 − £76·80 = ☐

Solve these word problems.

Count the pounds and pence separately to help you.

5 James buys a coat costing £32·79. How much change from £50 does he get?

6 Katie has saved £100 to buy a computer game. She finds the game online costing £66·37, including delivery. How much money will she have left to buy other things?

7 Deepa is buying fabric to make a special dress. The whole roll of fabric costs £100 but Deepa only buys part of it. She pays £43·64. What is the value of the fabric left on the roll?

THINK Sanjay bought two tickets, one for him and one for his dad. His dad's ticket was twice the price of his. He spent £39 in total. How much were the tickets?

I am confident with using Frog to complete subtractions.

How much money will each child have after buying a £62·75 ticket for a theme park?

① Liberty	② Piotr	③ Willow	④ Anjali

£75·90	£83·70	£92·45	£78·40

Answer these word problems.

⑤ Eva went to a football game and the ticket cost £28·35. She paid with two £20 notes. How much change did she get?

⑥ Kylie paid £42·78 for a dress online, including the postal cost. If the delivery cost £6·89, how much did the dress cost?

⑦ Steve wants to buy a computer game that costs £87·14. He has saved £76·87 and has a voucher for £5 off the game. How much more does he need to buy the game?

⑧ Mr Smith pays £69·32 for diesel for his car and some snacks at the petrol station. The snacks cost £2 for a drink and 85p for a chocolate bar. How much did the diesel cost?

THINK Abdul bought two identical tickets with £50 and was given £8·25 change. His friend Jim says that cannot be correct. He says that if the tickets are the same price then the change must be an even number of pence. Is he correct?

 I am confident with using Frog to complete money subtractions.

What is the difference between each pair of children's savings?

1. Emily £36·45   Sarah £28·79
2. Sam £45·36   David £36·84
3. Dinesh £75·14   Ella £64·66
4. Axil £67·33   Deepa £33·85

Solve these word problems.

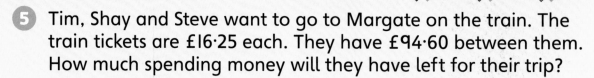

5. Tim, Shay and Steve want to go to Margate on the train. The train tickets are £16·25 each. They have £94·60 between them. How much spending money will they have left for their trip?

6. Leslie had £67·32 and spent £14·90. Keith had £44·68 and spent £3·75. Who has more money now, Leslie or Keith, and by how much?

7. Miss Lee had £42·65 and spent £36·44. She shared her change equally between her three daughters. How much did each daughter get?

8. Mrs Clark stayed in a hotel for two nights. The hotel cost £42·42 each night. How much change from £100 did she get?

9. Alan had £94·88 in his bank account. He withdrew £50 in cash and bought a pair of shoes with his debit card from the bank account for £28·75. How much money is left in his account now?

10. Hatem counted the money in his piggy bank. He had £28·74. He repaid his mum £10·50 that he owed her and he spent half of the rest on magazines. How much did he have left after that?

THINK Parvati bought three identical tickets with £60 and was given £7·75 change. Her friend Jill says that cannot be correct. She says that if the tickets are the same price then the change must be a multiple of 3. Is she correct?

I am confident with using Frog to complete money subtractions.

48

Multiplication using mental strategies

Write the first ten multiples of 6. Use doubling to write the first ten multiples of 12. Use doubling again to write the first ten multiples of 24.

Use your table facts to complete these multiplications.

1 3 × 24 = ☐   **3** 9 × 24 = ☐   **5** 8 × 24 = ☐

2 7 × 24 = ☐   **4** 6 × 24 = ☐   **6** 4 × 24 = ☐

These facts have been obtained by doubling.

1 × 13 = 13	1 × 16 = 16	1 × 15 = 15
2 × 13 = 26	2 × 16 = 32	2 × 15 = 30
4 × 13 = 52	4 × 16 = 64	4 × 15 = 60
8 × 13 = 104	8 × 16 = 128	8 × 15 = 120
16 × 13 = 208	16 × 16 = 256	16 × 15 = 240

Use the facts above to complete these multiplications.

7 3 × 13 = ☐   **12** 21 × 16 = ☐   **17** 17 × 13 = ☐   **22** 24 × 13 = ☐

8 12 × 16 = ☐   **13** 11 × 13 = ☐   **18** 17 × 17 = ☐   **23** 18 × 13 = ☐

9 5 × 13 = ☐   **14** 5 × 15 = ☐   **19** 13 × 13 = ☐   **24** 13 × 15 = ☐

10 3 × 15 = ☐   **15** 11 × 16 = ☐   **20** 6 × 15 = ☐   **25** 31 × 13 = ☐

11 7 × 13 = ☐   **16** 17 × 15 = ☐   **21** 16 × 25 = ☐   **26** 11 × 15 = ☐

 THINK Use doubling to create a table for × 17 facts. Use it to write at least five other really hard × 17 facts!

⦂ **I am confident with solving multiplications using mental strategies.**

Short multiplication and the grid method

These children used number cards to create a multiplication. They tried to get an answer close to 10 000. Predict the two nearest answers, then complete each child's multiplication to find out who was nearest, next nearest, and so on ...

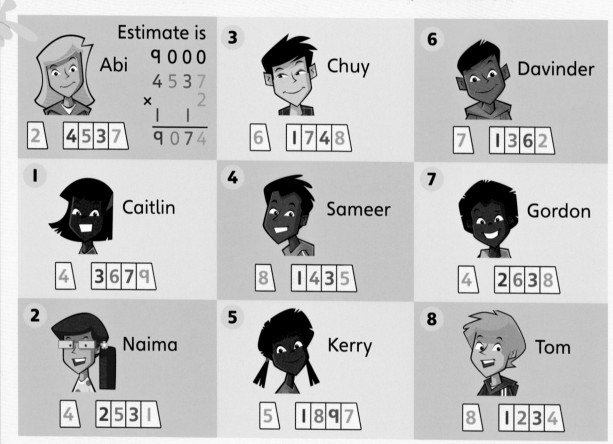

Abi — Estimate is 9000

$$\begin{array}{r} 4\,5\,3\,7 \\ \times\qquad 2 \\ \hline 9\,0\,7\,4 \end{array}$$

2 | 4537

3 — Chuy
6 | 1748

6 — Davinder
7 | 1362

1 — Caitlin
4 | 3679

4 — Sameer
8 | 1435

7 — Gordon
4 | 2638

2 — Naima
4 | 2531

5 — Kerry
5 | 1897

8 — Tom
8 | 1234

Arrange the digits to create these multiplications.

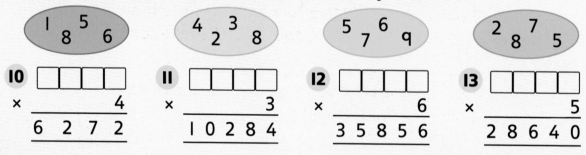

1 5 8 6

4 3 2 8

5 6 7 9

2 7 8 5

10
$$\begin{array}{r} \square\square\square\square \\ \times\qquad 4 \\ \hline 6\ 2\ 7\ 2 \end{array}$$

11
$$\begin{array}{r} \square\square\square\square \\ \times\qquad 3 \\ \hline 1\ 0\ 2\ 8\ 4 \end{array}$$

12
$$\begin{array}{r} \square\square\square\square \\ \times\qquad 6 \\ \hline 3\ 5\ 8\ 5\ 6 \end{array}$$

13
$$\begin{array}{r} \square\square\square\square \\ \times\qquad 5 \\ \hline 2\ 8\ 6\ 4\ 0 \end{array}$$

THINK Can you create a multiplication like this, $\square \times \square\square\square\square$, so that the digits in the answer are in ascending or descending order, e.g. 1369 or 9421? The multiplier cannot be 1!

○
○ **I am confident with using short multiplication.**
○

Solve these problems using the method shown.

1 How much for six packs of sausages that cost £5·79 each?

6 × £5·79 =

×	£5	70p	9p	
6	£30	£4·20	54p	= ☐

2 How much for four packs of onions that cost £3·68 each?

4 × £3·68 =

×			
			= ☐

3 How much for three packs of burgers that cost £4·57 each?

4 How much for six packs of veggie bites that cost £2·69 each?

5 How much for five packs of rolls that cost £1·93 each?

6 How much for four packs of potatoes that cost £2·88 each?

Solve these word problems using the same method.

7 How much change from £20 will James get if he buys six packs of potatoes that cost £2·88 each?

8 Kim buys five packs of veggie bites for £2·69 each. How much change from £20 will she get?

9 Mrs Richardson is having a bonfire party. She buys eight boxes of fireworks for £5·75 each. How much change from £50 will she get?

●
○ **I am confident with using grid multiplication.**
○

Look at this table of firework prices. Work out the total cost using short multiplication.

1

Price per box	Number of boxes needed	Total cost
£21·13	4	
£17·23	3	
£18·61	5	
£14·87	3	
£29·95	9	
£39·84	4	

Answer these word problems.

2 Three boxes of burgers cost £12·45 each. Find the change from £50.

3 You buy two large bags of potatoes at £11·79 each and three packs of bread rolls at £13·35 each. How much do you spend altogether?

4 Rockets cost £13·69 for a box of six or £40·99 for a box of 18. Is it better value to buy three of the boxes of six or the box of 18? How much would you save buying the cheaper option rather than the more expensive option?

5 Mr Collins is organising a large bonfire party and has £73·26 to buy giant sparklers for all the children. Packs of giant sparklers cost £11·38 for eight. If he buys 48 giant sparklers, how much money will he have left afterwards?

I am confident with using short multiplication.

Look at this table of firework prices. Work out the total cost using short multiplication.

1.

Price per box	Number of boxes needed	Total cost
£22·79	6	
£37·88	7	
£18·61	8	
£14·87	7	
£49·74	9	
£57·86	8	

Answer these word problems.

2. For a large bonfire party Mr Franks buys five large bags of potatoes at £11·79 each and six rolls of tin-foil at £3·86 each. How much did he pay altogether?

3. Six boxes of burgers cost £12·45 each. Find the change from £100.

4. Chloe buys seven packs of premium burgers that cost £13·78 each and the shop gives her an £8 discount. She pays with £100 in cash. How much change is she given?

5. Jamie's shopping receipt shows that he has bought four items costing £11·67 each, five items costing £5·79 each and six items costing £3·73. How much change from £100 did he receive? How much change is she given?

 Is £43·60 × 5 more than £34·50 × 6? Decide, then check by multiplying both!

I am confident with using short multiplication.

Long multiplication and the grid method

Solve these multiplications.

1 324 × 14 = ☐

×	300	20	4
10	3000	200	40
4	1200	80	16

2 513 × 12 = ☐

×	500	10	3
10			
2			

3 625 × 13 = ☐

×	600	20	5
10			
3			

4 242 × 14 = ☐

5 146 × 12 = ☐

6 453 × 13 = ☐

THINK   345 × 1☐ = 4830. What is the missing digit?

● I am confident with using grid multiplication.
○
○

Estimate first and then solve these multiplications using long multiplication.

$$
\begin{array}{r}
3\ 4\ 8 \\
\times\quad 1\ 6 \\
\hline
3\ 4\ 8\ 0 \\
2\ 0\ 8\ 8 \\
\hline
5\ 5\ 6\ 8
\end{array}
$$

1 573 × 15 = ☐

2 246 × 14 = ☐

3 437 × 18 = ☐

4 825 × 19 = ☐

5 1546 × 13 = ☐

6 7846 × 16 = ☐

7 5206 × 12 = ☐

8 8564 × 17 = ☐

Estimate first to help you know if your answer is reasonable.

 Is 345 × 16 going to have a larger answer than 346 × 15? Write your estimate first, then work it out.

● I am confident with using long multiplication.

Estimate first and then solve these multiplications.

1 2445 × 16 = ☐

2 5738 × 17 = ☐

3 7957 × 14 = ☐

4 1745 × 19 = ☐

5 9753 × 18 = ☐

6 7685 × 16 = ☐

7 2854 × 13 = ☐

8 6875 × 17 = ☐

9 Which of these multiplications has an answer closest to 75 000?

4433 × 17 = ☐

4175 × 18 = ☐

3896 × 19 = ☐

 How many hours are there in a year?

I am confident with using long multiplication.

Choose a number from each set to multiply together. Use the grid method. Do this three times.

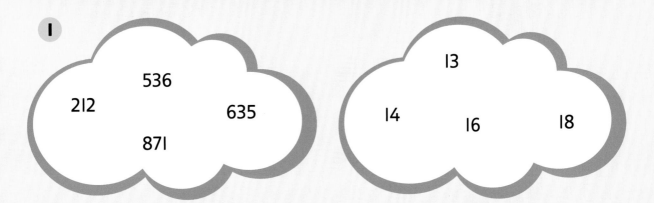

1

536
212
635
871

13
14
16
18

Choose a number from each set to multiply together. Use the grid method. Do this three times.

2

698
377
117
451

14
15
12
13

 The same digit number is in each of the boxes. What is it?

3 ☐ 2 × 1 ☐ = 5792

● I am confident with using grid multiplication.

Estimate then work out which of the multiplications is closest to 70 000.

1 Abigail

Estimate is
6 0 0 0 0

6 5 3 7
×   1 2
———

| 1 2 | | 6 | 5 | 3 | 7 |

3 Naima

| 2 | 4 | | 3 | 5 | 3 | 1 |

5 Sameer

| 1 | 8 | | 2 | 0 | 3 | 5 |

2 Caitlin

| 2 | 4 | | 2 | 6 | 7 | 9 |

4 Chuy

| 3 | 9 | | 1 | 7 | 4 | 8 |

6 Kerry

| 1 | 7 | | 3 | 8 | 9 | 7 |

 THINK   The same digit number is in each of the boxes. What is it?

6 ☐ 7 × 1 ☐ = 10 672

I am confident with using long multiplication.

Negative numbers

 GRAB! **Number line resource sheet with negative and positive numbers**

Find the difference between each pair of temperatures.

1 –3 °C and 4 °C

4 –11 °C and –7 °C

2 –15 °C and –9 °C

5 –4 °C and 9 °C

3 –5 °C and 6 °C

6 –12 °C and –3 °C

Write these numbers in order from the lowest to the greatest.

7 5·7, –3·8, –12

10 –0·7, 0·8, –1

8 –6·3, –9, 2·1

11 3·4, –16, –9·9

9 –1·8, 7, –6·4

12 7·9, –8, –7·8

Answer these word problems.

13 The temperature in Moscow was 4 °C.
The temperature dropped by 9 °C overnight.
What was the lowest temperature overnight?

14 The temperature in London was –3 °C.
The temperature rose by 14 °C by midday.
What was the temperature at midday?

 THINK The difference between a positive and a negative number is 5. What pairs of numbers could they be?

○
○ **I am confident with reading and ordering negative**
○ **numbers.**

Find the difference between each pair of temperatures.

1 −5 °C and −12 °C

2 7 °C and −14 °C

3 −8 °C and 13 °C

4 −7 °C and −22 °C

5 16 °C and −9 °C

6 −12 °C and −31 °C

Write these numbers in order from the lowest to the greatest.

7 −4·82, 3·25, 5·12, −7·26

8 −3·62, −9·32, 10·44, −5·76

9 6·71, −6·71, 7·16, −1·76

10 2·02, −2·22, 2·20, −2

11 −5·5, 5·55, 5·5, −5·55

12 8·81, −8·88, −8·11, 8·01

Answer these word problems.

13 The temperature at ground level in Helsinki is 20 °C lower than in London. The temperature in a basement flat in Helsinki is 5 °C below the temperature at ground level. If it is −29 °C in the basement, what is the temperature in London?

14 The temperature in Mrs Jones' fridge is 3 °C. The temperature in her freezer is normally 21 °C colder than in the fridge. Mrs Jones has unfortunately left her freezer door slightly open and the temperature in her freezer has risen by 8 °C. What is its current temperature?

 The difference between a positive and a negative number is 10. The digit value of the positive number is greater than the digit value of the negative number. What pairs of numbers could they be?

○
○ **I am confident with reading and ordering negative**
○ **numbers.**

Look at the temperature table for London. Answer the questions about the temperatures.

GRAB! Resource sheet with a thermometer or vertical positive and negative number line.

Month	Average temperature (°C)
January	–3
February	–1
March	0
April	9
May	16
June	18
July	26
August	28
September	20
October	11
November	5
December	–2

1. How many degrees colder is the average temperature in September than in August?

2. In which month is the average temperature 2 °C warmer than the average temperature for January?

3. How many degrees difference is there between the average temperature for January and the average temperature for April?

4. In which month is the average temperature 17 °C warmer than the average temperature for February?

5. Find the difference between the average temperature in July and the average temperature for December.

6. In which month is the average temperature 20 °C warmer than the average temperature for December?

I am confident with reading and ordering negative numbers.

Look at the table showing the melting points for different elements. Answer the questions about melting points.

Element	Melting point (°C)
bromine	−7
mercury	−39
chlorine	−101
nitrogen	−210
oxygen	−218
potassium	64
sodium	98
tin	232

1. What is the degree difference between the melting points of bromine and sodium?

2. Which element has a melting point that is 165 °C colder than the melting point of potassium?

3. Which element has a melting point that is 271 °C warmer than the melting point of mercury?

4. What is the degree difference between the melting points of oxygen and nitrogen?

Write the pairs of elements that have the following differences.

5. 34 °C   6. 109 °C   7. 199 °C   8. 137 °C

Answer these word problems.

9. Rachel has a balance of −£76·20 in her bank account and she gets paid £120·50. How much does she have in her account now?

10. Leo has £27·30 in his account but pays a bill for £59·35 from the account. By how much is he now overdrawn?

THINK Ibraheem subtracts one negative number from another and gets an answer of −1. If one of Ibraheem's numbers is −6, what two possible numbers could the other be?

I am confident with reading and ordering negative numbers.

Comparing fractions

GRAB! Fraction strips from a resource sheet.

Write < or > between each pair of fractions.

Remember to make both fractions have the same larger denominator – find the equivalent fraction for the fraction with the smaller denominator.

$\frac{3}{4} < \frac{7}{8}$ because $\frac{3}{4} = \frac{6}{8}$

1. $\frac{3}{8} \square \frac{1}{4}$

2. $\frac{7}{12} \square \frac{3}{4}$

3. $\frac{5}{6} \square \frac{2}{3}$

4. $\frac{3}{4} \square \frac{5}{8}$

5. $\frac{1}{3} \square \frac{4}{9}$

6. $\frac{1}{2} \square \frac{3}{5}$

7. $\frac{4}{5} \square \frac{9}{10}$

8. $\frac{5}{9} \square \frac{2}{3}$

9. $\frac{3}{10} \square \frac{2}{5}$

10. $\frac{7}{8} \square \frac{3}{4}$

11. $\frac{7}{10} \square \frac{67}{100}$

12. $\frac{5}{6} \square \frac{11}{12}$

13. $\frac{8}{10} \square \frac{71}{100}$

14. $\frac{39}{100} \square \frac{4}{10}$

15. $\frac{9}{10} \square \frac{19}{20}$

THINK How many ways can you write $\frac{2}{5}$? Find at least eight ways.

I am confident with comparing fractions.

GRAB! Fraction strips from a resource sheet.

1. $\frac{3}{4}$ ☐ $\frac{6}{12}$

2. $\frac{3}{16}$ ☐ $\frac{1}{4}$

3. $\frac{4}{5}$ ☐ $\frac{7}{10}$

4. $\frac{2}{5}$ ☐ $\frac{9}{20}$

5. $\frac{7}{8}$ ☐ $\frac{23}{24}$

6. $\frac{5}{7}$ ☐ $\frac{11}{14}$

7. $\frac{5}{9}$ ☐ $\frac{2}{3}$

8. $\frac{52}{100}$ ☐ $\frac{6}{10}$

9. $\frac{6}{10}$ ☐ $\frac{2}{5}$

10. $\frac{37}{100}$ ☐ $\frac{2}{5}$

11. $\frac{19}{100}$ ☐ $\frac{2}{10}$

12. $\frac{4}{5}$ ☐ $\frac{88}{100}$

13. $\frac{3}{10}$ ☐ $\frac{1}{20}$

14. $\frac{2}{3}$ ☐ $\frac{3}{5}$

15. $\frac{3}{4}$ ☐ $\frac{5}{6}$

16. $\frac{4}{5}$ ☐ $\frac{3}{4}$

THINK Lucy and Harry have each written a fraction. If Lucy's fraction is larger by $\frac{1}{8}$, what could their fractions be?

I am confident with reading and comparing fractions.

1. $\dfrac{1}{2} \square \dfrac{5}{8}$

2. $\dfrac{1}{4} \square \dfrac{3}{8}$

3. $\dfrac{1}{2} \square \dfrac{3}{8}$

4. $\dfrac{1}{3} \square \dfrac{2}{9}$

5. $\dfrac{5}{6} \square \dfrac{2}{3}$

6. $\dfrac{7}{9} \square \dfrac{2}{3}$

7. $\dfrac{3}{10} \square \dfrac{1}{2}$

8. $\dfrac{3}{5} \square \dfrac{7}{10}$

9. $\dfrac{7}{10} \square \dfrac{1}{2}$

 THINK How could we find out which is larger, $\dfrac{3}{4}$ or $\dfrac{2}{3}$?

I am confident with reading and comparing fractions.

65

1. Write two fractions with related denominators.

   e.g. $\frac{3}{4}$ and $\frac{7}{8}$, or $\frac{2}{3}$ and $\frac{8}{9}$, or $\frac{4}{5}$ and $\frac{9}{10}$

2. Make sure both fractions are the largest fraction that it is possible to write without writing one whole.

   e.g. You write $\frac{7}{8}$ because $\frac{8}{8}$ is one whole

3. Compare the two fractions by converting the one with the smaller denominator to an equivalent fraction with the larger denominator.

   e.g. $\frac{4}{5} = \frac{8}{10}$, so $\frac{8}{10} < \frac{9}{10}$

4. Repeat this with different pairs of related fractions. Write at least ten different pairs.

5. Write two fractions with related denominators, but make sure you write the unit fraction of each type – so the numerator is 1.

   e.g. $\frac{1}{5}$ and $\frac{1}{10}$

6. Again, compare the fractions by converting the one with the smaller denominator to an equivalent fraction with the larger denominator.

   e.g. $\frac{1}{5} = \frac{2}{10}$, so $\frac{2}{10} > \frac{1}{10}$

7. Again, repeat this to write and compare at least ten different pairs of related fractions.

I am confident with reading and comparing fractions.

Fractions and mixed numbers

Convert these mixed numbers and simplify them where possible.

$$\frac{11}{14} + \frac{5}{14} = \frac{16}{14} = 1\frac{2}{14} = 1\frac{1}{7}$$

1. $\frac{5}{6} + \frac{5}{6} = \square$

2. $\frac{5}{9} + \frac{7}{9} = \square$

3. $\frac{5}{8} + \frac{7}{8} = \square$

4. $\frac{3}{10} + \frac{9}{10} = \square$

5. $\frac{7}{12} + \frac{11}{12} = \square$

6. $\frac{7}{9} + \frac{5}{9} + \frac{7}{9} = \square$

7. $\frac{3}{8} + \frac{5}{8} + \frac{7}{8} = \square$

8. $\frac{5}{12} + \frac{11}{12} + \frac{7}{12} = \square$

9. $\frac{7}{15} + \frac{11}{15} + \frac{2}{15} = \square$

10. $\frac{5}{10} + \frac{3}{10} + \frac{9}{10} = \square$

THINK Hannah says that two fractions were added and the total was a mixed number greater than 2. Claire says this is not possible. Who is right?

○ **I am confident with converting and simplifying fractions.**
○
○

Area and perimeter

Calculate the area and perimeter for each shape.
Give your answers in m and m².

1

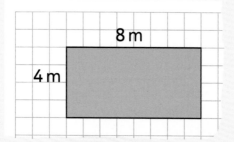

8 m

4 m

2

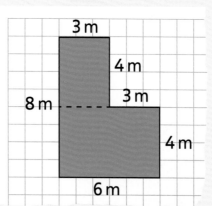

3 m

4 m

8 m

3 m

4 m

6 m

3

3 m

10 m

4

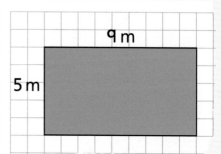

9 m

5 m

5

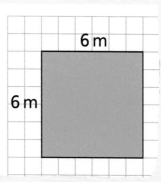

6 m

6 m

6

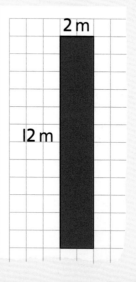

2 m

12 m

THINK Two different rectangles both have an area of 24 cm².
Will the perimeters be the same? How do you know?

○
○ I am confident with working out the area and perimeter
○ of shapes.

Calculate the area and perimeter for each shape.
Give your answers in cm and cm².

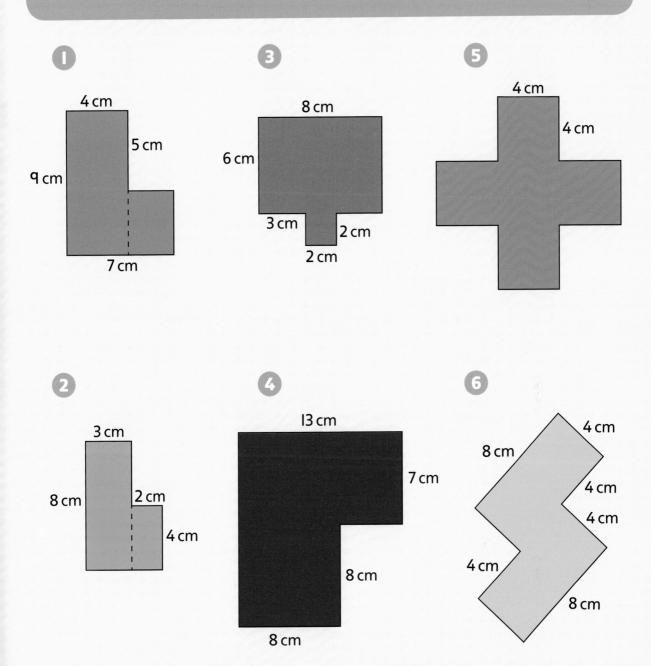

1

4 cm
5 cm
9 cm
7 cm

3

8 cm
6 cm
3 cm
2 cm
2 cm

5

4 cm
4 cm

2

3 cm
8 cm
2 cm
4 cm

4

13 cm
7 cm
8 cm
8 cm

6

4 cm
8 cm
4 cm
4 cm
4 cm
8 cm

THINK

Two different L-shapes both have an area of 22 cm². They have different perimeters. Can you draw them?

I am confident with working out the area and perimeter of shapes.

69

Finding volume

Calculate the volume of each shape.

Volume = length × width × height

$V = l \times w \times h$

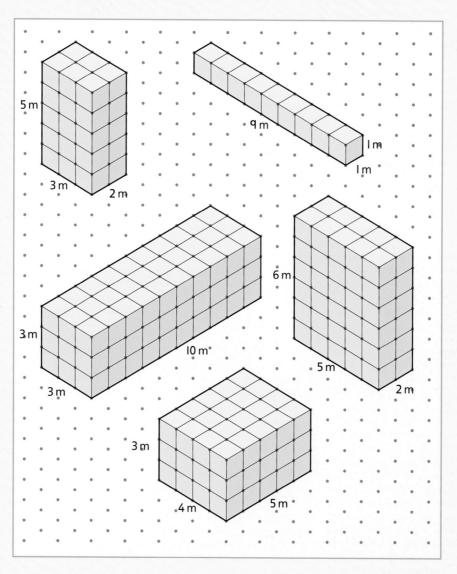

① 3 m × 2 m = 6 m²

6 m² × 5 m = ☐ m³

THINK   A box has a volume of 36 cm³. The height is 6 cm².
What lengths could the length and width of the base be?

○
○ **I am confident with working out the volume of shapes.**
○

Calculate the volume of each shape.

Volume = length × width × height
$V = l \times w \times h$

Remember to use m³ or cm³.

1

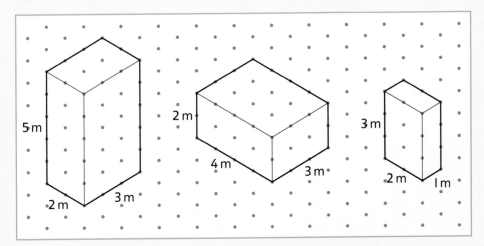

5 m   2 m   3 m
2 m   4 m   3 m   2 m   1 m
3 m   3 m

2

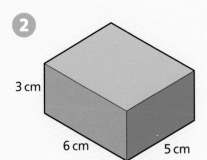

3 cm
6 cm   5 cm

4

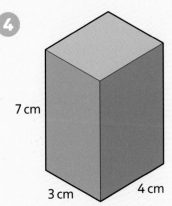

7 cm
3 cm   4 cm

6

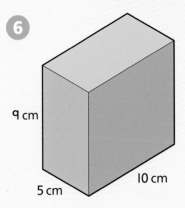

9 cm
5 cm   10 cm

3

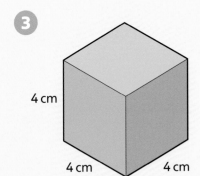

4 cm
4 cm   4 cm

5

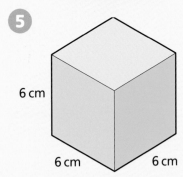

6 cm
6 cm   6 cm

 THINK   Square numbers are numbers multiplied by themselves. What are cube numbers? Can you write the first three cube numbers?

I am confident with working out the volume of shapes.

Calculating area

Calculate the area of each triangle.

Area = $\frac{1}{2}$ base × height

$A = \frac{1}{2} b \times h$

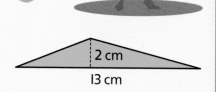

Remember to give your answers in cm² or m².

1

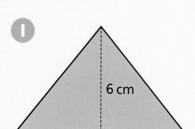

6 cm

10 cm

4

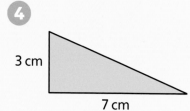

3 cm

7 cm

7

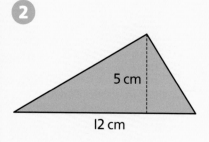

2 cm

13 cm

2

5 cm

12 cm

5

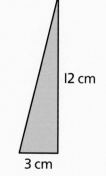

12 cm

3 cm

8

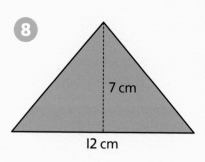

7 cm

12 cm

3

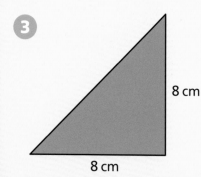

8 cm

8 cm

6

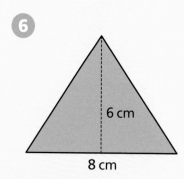

6 cm

8 cm

9

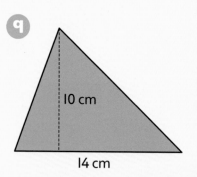

10 cm

14 cm

THINK   A triangle has an area of 24 cm². If the height is 4 cm, what is its base?

○
○   **I am confident with working out the area of triangles.**
○

72

Calculate the area of each parallelogram.

Area = base × height
$A = b \times h$

Check your answers by counting the squares.

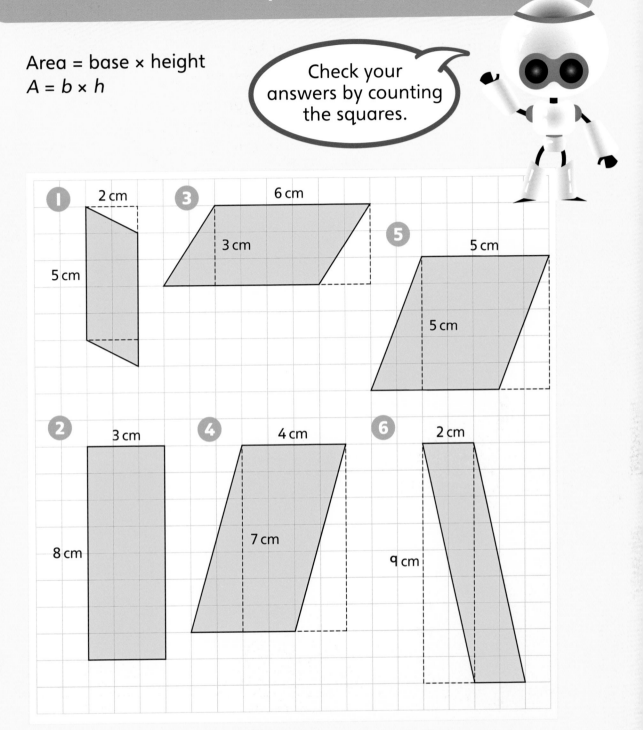

1. 2 cm, 5 cm

3. 6 cm, 3 cm

5. 5 cm, 5 cm

2. 3 cm, 8 cm

4. 4 cm, 7 cm

6. 2 cm, 9 cm

 THINK Draw a parallelogram on squared paper and find its area. Draw a diagonal. Can you calculate the area of each triangle created?

I am confident with working out the area of parallelograms.

Calculate the area of each of these shapes.

Area of a triangle = $\frac{1}{2} b \times h$
Area of a parallelogram = $b \times h$

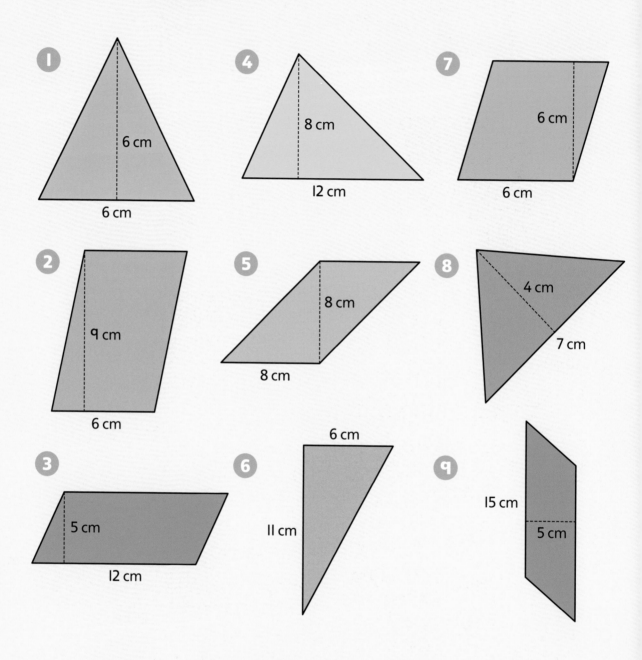

1
6 cm
6 cm

2
9 cm
6 cm

3
5 cm
12 cm

4
8 cm
12 cm

5
8 cm
8 cm

6
6 cm
11 cm

7
6 cm
6 cm

8
4 cm
7 cm

9
15 cm
5 cm

 THINK A triangle has an area of 18 cm².
If the base is 12 cm, what is the height?

○
○ **I am confident with working out the area of triangles**
○ **and parallelograms.**

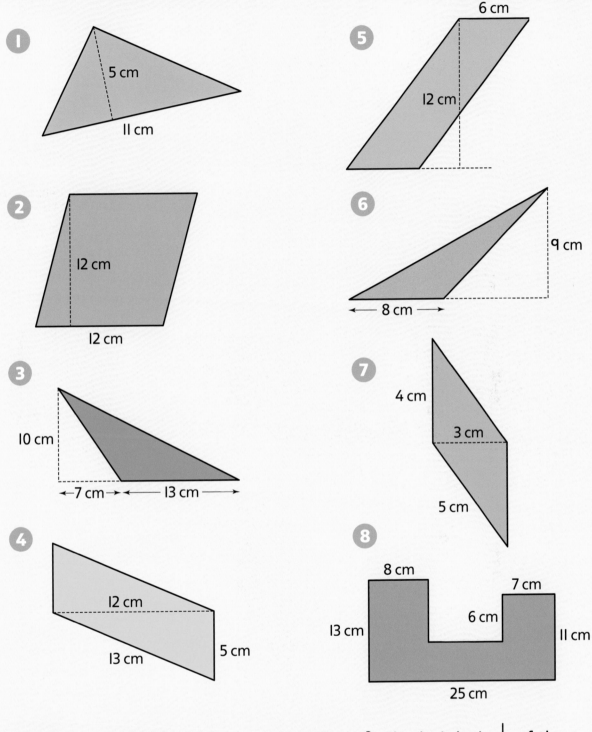

1 5 cm 11 cm

2 12 cm 12 cm

3 10 cm ←7 cm→←— 13 cm —→

4 12 cm 13 cm 5 cm

5 6 cm 12 cm

6 9 cm ←— 8 cm —→

7 4 cm 3 cm 5 cm

8 8 cm 7 cm 13 cm 6 cm 11 cm 25 cm

THINK A triangle has an area of 18 cm². The height is $\frac{1}{4}$ of the length of the base. What whole numbers could the lengths of the base and height be?

Nets

Write the name of the shape made by each net.
Do they all make closed 3d shapes?

1

4

7

2

5

8

3

6

9 Draw a net for a tetrahedron.

THINK Draw a net for a shape that is not possible.
Explain why it does not work.

I am confident with drawing and interpreting nets.

Dividing by whole numbers

Solve these divisions, using the function machines to help you.

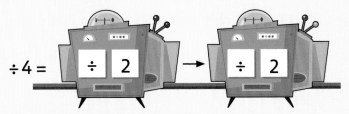

$\div 4 =$

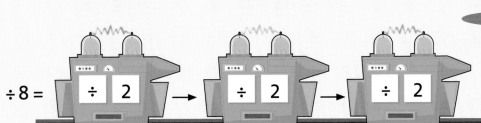

$\div 8 =$

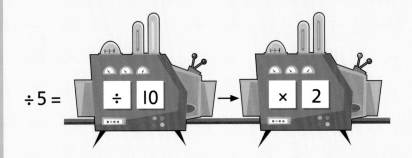

$\div 5 =$

1. $448 \div 4 = \square$
2. $320 \div 5 = \square$
3. $148 \div 4 = \square$
4. $600 \div 8 = \square$
5. $126 \div 4 = \square$

6. $456 \div 8 = \square$
7. $370 \div 5 = \square$
8. $920 \div 8 = \square$
9. $616 \div 4 = \square$
10. $180 \div 8 = \square$

THINK For each group of function machines, think of one function machine which changes the output back into the input.

I am confident with dividing by 4, 5 and 8.

Solve these divisions.

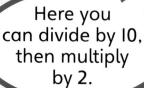

Remember you can halve three times to divide by 8.

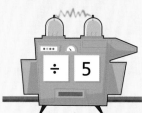

Here you can divide by 10, then multiply by 2.

Remember you can divide by 2, then divide by 10.

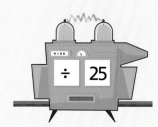

Here you can divide by 100, then times by 4.

1. 448 ÷ 8 = ☐
2. 390 ÷ 5 = ☐
3. 840 ÷ 20 = ☐
4. 600 ÷ 25 = ☐
5. 252 ÷ 8 = ☐

6. 325 ÷ 5 = ☐
7. 3000 ÷ 25 = ☐
8. 422 ÷ 20 = ☐
9. 616 ÷ 8 = ☐
10. 1200 ÷ 25 = ☐

 Devise a pair of function machines to divide by 50 and a pair to divide by 250.

● **I am confident with dividing by 5, 8, 20 and 25.**

Use short division to find the answers. Divide the remainders to give fractions. Simplify the fractions where you can.

1 6 ⟌ 748

4 7 ⟌ 9248

7 8 ⟌ 4204

2 4 ⟌ 586

5 3 ⟌ 4756

8 7 ⟌ 5785

3 9 ⟌ 586

6 6 ⟌ 7041

9 9 ⟌ 2865

Use short division to find the answers to these in the same way.

10 6869 ÷ 7 = ☐

11 6183 ÷ 8 = ☐

 THINK A mystery 4-digit number with three digits the same and a zero in the tens place is divided by 5. There is a remainder of 4. What two possible numbers could it be?

I am confident with using short division and giving remainders as fractions.

Use short division to find the answers. Divide the remainders to give fractions. Simplify the fractions where you can.

① 7407 ÷ 6 = ☐

② 2423 ÷ 7 = ☐

③ 8746 ÷ 4 = ☐

④ 5182 ÷ 8 = ☐

⑤ 2273 ÷ 7 = ☐

⑥ 4118 ÷ 9 = ☐

⑦ 6522 ÷ 8 = ☐

⑧ 4988 ÷ 9 = ☐

⑨ 8324 ÷ 6 = ☐

⑩ 3170 ÷ 8 = ☐

⑪ 9151 ÷ 4 = ☐

⑫ 4126 ÷ 6 = ☐

⑬ 2766 ÷ 8 = ☐

⑭ 4799 ÷ 7 = ☐

 THINK

2 3 4 6 8 9

If you divide a mystery 4-digit number by any of these values there is no remainder. What is the mystery number?

I am confident with using short division and giving remainders as fractions.

Solve these divisions.

1   3) 948

4   8) 896

7   5) 387

2   4) 564

5   3) 771

8   4) 8565

3   5) 785

6   6) 852

9   3) 2469

Follow these instructions and look for patterns.

10

Divide 123 by 6.

Divide 234 by 6.

Divide 345 by 6.

Keep following the pattern, dividing 456, 567, 678, 789 and 891 by 6.

What do you notice about the patterns of the remainders?

Try dividing each of the same numbers by 3 and see if you notice anything.

Solve these divisions.

1 2072 ÷ 6 = ☐

4 8236 ÷ 8 = ☐

2 2002 ÷ 7 = ☐

5 2764 ÷ 9 = ☐

3 2727 ÷ 4 = ☐

6 7253 ÷ 6 = ☐

Follow these instructions and look for patterns.

7

Divide 1101 by 6. Give the answer as a fraction.

Divide 2202 by 6. Give the answer as a fraction.

Divide 3303 by 6. Give the answer as a fraction.

Keep going like this up to and including 9909 ÷ 6.

Explain the pattern you find in the answers.

Explore other similar patterns in the same way.

Remember your divisibility rules for 3!

I am confident with using short division and giving remainders as fractions.

Addition and subtraction of fractions

$\frac{1}{2}$						$\frac{1}{2}$					
$\frac{1}{3}$				$\frac{1}{3}$				$\frac{1}{3}$			
$\frac{1}{4}$			$\frac{1}{4}$			$\frac{1}{4}$			$\frac{1}{4}$		
$\frac{1}{5}$		$\frac{1}{5}$		$\frac{1}{5}$		$\frac{1}{5}$			$\frac{1}{5}$		
$\frac{1}{6}$		$\frac{1}{6}$		$\frac{1}{6}$		$\frac{1}{6}$		$\frac{1}{6}$		$\frac{1}{6}$	
$\frac{1}{8}$		$\frac{1}{8}$	$\frac{1}{8}$		$\frac{1}{8}$		$\frac{1}{8}$		$\frac{1}{8}$	$\frac{1}{8}$	$\frac{1}{8}$
$\frac{1}{10}$	$\frac{1}{10}$	$\frac{1}{10}$	$\frac{1}{10}$	$\frac{1}{10}$	$\frac{1}{10}$	$\frac{1}{10}$	$\frac{1}{10}$	$\frac{1}{10}$	$\frac{1}{10}$		
$\frac{1}{12}$	$\frac{1}{12}$	$\frac{1}{12}$	$\frac{1}{12}$	$\frac{1}{12}$	$\frac{1}{12}$	$\frac{1}{12}$	$\frac{1}{12}$	$\frac{1}{12}$	$\frac{1}{12}$	$\frac{1}{12}$	$\frac{1}{12}$

Add these fractions.

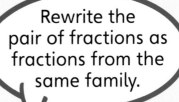

Rewrite the pair of fractions as fractions from the same family.

1. $\frac{1}{4} + \frac{1}{8} = \square$

2. $\frac{1}{3} + \frac{1}{6} = \square$

3. $\frac{1}{12} + \frac{1}{6} = \square$

4. $\frac{1}{10} + \frac{1}{5} = \square$

5. $\frac{1}{2} + \frac{1}{6} = \square$

6. $\frac{1}{2} + \frac{1}{10} = \square$

7. $\frac{1}{2} + \frac{1}{8} = \square$

8. $\frac{1}{2} + \frac{1}{3} = \square$

9. $\frac{1}{2} + \frac{1}{5} = \square$

10. $\frac{1}{3} + \frac{1}{8} = \square$

 Cat says that a pair of unit fractions (fractions with 1 at the top) can never have a total of 1. What do you think?

I am confident with adding fractions with different denominators.

1 $\frac{1}{3} + \frac{1}{4} = \square$

2 $\frac{1}{5} + \frac{1}{3} = \square$

3 $\frac{1}{2} + \frac{1}{5} = \square$

Choose pairs of these fractions to add together. Write at least six additions.

4

Write an addition of three fractions with a total of less than $\frac{1}{2}$.

○
○ **I am confident with adding fractions.**
○

Subtract these fractions, using the fraction strips to help you.

 **GRAB!** Fraction strips.

1. $\frac{1}{2} - \frac{1}{3} = \Box$

2. $\frac{1}{3} - \frac{1}{4} = \Box$

3. $\frac{1}{2} - \frac{1}{5} = \Box$

Subtract these fractions.

Rewrite the pair of fractions as fractions from the same family.

4. $\frac{1}{2} - \frac{1}{4} = \Box$

5. $\frac{1}{2} - \frac{1}{8} = \Box$

6. $\frac{1}{2} - \frac{1}{6} = \Box$

7. $\frac{1}{3} - \frac{1}{6} = \Box$

8. $\frac{1}{4} - \frac{1}{8} = \Box$

9. $\frac{1}{5} - \frac{1}{10} = \Box$

○ **I am confident with subtracting fractions.**
○
○

85

Fractions and percentages

1 **Find the matching pairs of fractions and percentages.**

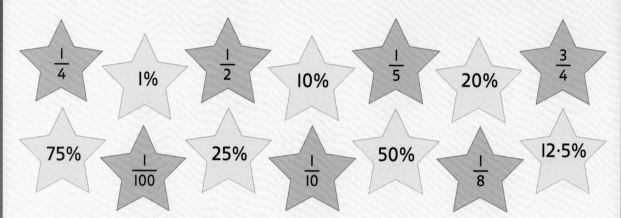

$\frac{1}{4}$ 1% $\frac{1}{2}$ 10% $\frac{1}{5}$ 20% $\frac{3}{4}$

75% $\frac{1}{100}$ 25% $\frac{1}{10}$ 50% $\frac{1}{8}$ 12·5%

Find 10% of each of these numbers. Use your answer for each to find 20%, 15% and 40% of the same numbers.

2 360

4 250

3 420

5 680

Find 50% of each of these numbers. Use your answer for each to find 25% and 75%.

6 480

8 280

7 520

9 720

THINK How could we find 67% of 300? Work this out with a partner. Compare this to $\frac{2}{3}$ of 300.

 **I am confident with finding equivalent fractions and percentages.**

Copy and complete this table.

1.

Fraction	$\frac{1}{2}$		$\frac{1}{10}$	$\frac{1}{5}$	$\frac{2}{5}$	$\frac{3}{10}$		$\frac{4}{5}$		$\frac{3}{4}$	$\frac{1}{8}$
Percentage	50%	25%					70%	1%		60%	

Below are the populations of some villages and the percentage of people who want a wind farm to be built. Write how many people in each village want a wind farm.

2. Banners Gate
Population: 1800
31% say yes

3. Boldmere
Population: 1400
21% say yes

4. Aldridge
Population: 1200
26% say yes

5. Four Oaks
Population: 800
52% say yes

6. Wylde Green
Population: 700
29% say yes

7. New Oscott
Population: 1100
43% say yes

8. Streetly
Population: 900
38% say yes

9. Minworth
Population: 600
46% say yes

 The newspaper says that 67% of people in a village want the wind farm. In fact, $\frac{2}{3}$ of people want it. What is the difference between these numbers if there are 3000 people in the village?

I am confident with finding equivalent fractions and percentages.

Match the fractions and percentages.

1

1%   75%
                30%
10%   25%
    50%   20%

$\frac{1}{10}$ $\frac{1}{100}$ $\frac{1}{4}$
          $\frac{3}{10}$ $\frac{1}{5}$
$\frac{3}{4}$ $\frac{3}{10}$
          $\frac{1}{2}$

Work out the percentages of these amounts of money.

2 10% of £24   20% of £24   55% of £24

3 10% of £36   20% of £36   5% of £36

4 10% of £50   1% of £50   11% of £50

5 10% of £42   1% of £42   11% of £42

6 50% of £84   25% of £84   75% of £84

7 50% of £72   25% of £72   75% of £72

 If 1% of the total money in Sam's piggybank is £3·50, how much has he saved?

○
○ **I am confident with finding equivalent fractions and**
○ **percentages.**

88

Answer these questions.

Find 10% of the amount. Use this to find the percentage given.

①
30% of £12

④
40% of £16

⑦
30% of £19

⑩
20% of £17

②
40% of £14

⑤
20% of £27

⑧
40% of £23

⑪
40% of £38

③
30% of £15

⑥
60% of £22

⑨
30% of £42

⑫
30% of £29

⑬ 15% of £80 = ☐

⑭ 35% of £60 = ☐

⑮ 90% of £11 = ☐

⑯ 95% of £12 = ☐

Find 10% and use it to help you find the answers.

 THINK Can you find 10% of $\frac{1}{2}$ of 500? What would be an easier calculation which would give the same answer?

 I am confident with finding equivalent fractions and percentages.

1

Item	Original price	10% discount	Sale price
Electric mixer	£45	£4.50	£40.50
Toaster	£18		
Kettle	£32		

2

Item	Original price	25% discount	Sale price
Coffee maker	£56		
Blender	£42		
Grill	£39		

3

Item	Original price	15% discount	Sale price
Water purifier	£35		
Slow cooker	£52		
Waffle maker	£47		

 THINK An item was reduced by 10%. Its new price is £45. What was its original price?

I am confident with finding percentages of amounts of money.

1. Which is greater and by how much: $\frac{2}{5}$ of £65 or 15% of £170?

2. Which number is exactly halfway between $\frac{2}{7}$ of 35 cm and 4% of 700 cm?

3. If a shop sells items at 75% of the original prices, how much would you pay for a TV with an original price of £360?

4. Jasper spends 34% of his day sleeping, 26% at school, 10% watching television and 5% eating. How many hours does he have left for other activities?

5. Sam won £800. He chose to give 40% of the amount to charity and $\frac{1}{4}$ of the amount to his son. How much was he left with and what percentage of the amount was this?

6. In a book sale, all books have 10% off. Natalie bought four books with original prices of £4·50, £1·60, £12·80 and £3·40. How much did she save?

7. Rani is given interest payments of 11% of the money in her savings account. She has £720 in her account. How much interest is she paid?

8. An ice cream maker costs £35 in a shop. Joanne can buy it 15% cheaper online. How much does it cost online?

Multiplying and converting fractions

Copy and complete this multiplication grid.

1.

×	$\frac{1}{2}$	$\frac{1}{4}$	$\frac{3}{4}$	$\frac{1}{3}$	$\frac{2}{3}$	$\frac{2}{5}$
1						
2	1			$\frac{2}{3}$		
3						
4				$1\frac{1}{3}$		
5			$3\frac{3}{4}$			
6					4	
7		$1\frac{3}{4}$				
8						
9					6	
10						
11		$2\frac{3}{4}$				
12						$4\frac{4}{5}$

THINK Look for some multiplications that have the same answer. Write some more with the same answer.

I am confident with multiplying and converting fractions.

Answer these word problems.

1 Three children each eat $\frac{2}{3}$ of a cake.
How much cake is eaten altogether?

2 Three children each eat $\frac{2}{5}$ of a cherry flan.
How much flan is eaten altogether?

3 Three children each eat $\frac{3}{4}$ of a custard pie.
How much custard pie is eaten altogether?

Answer these word problems. Write your answers as mixed numbers.

4 Two children each eat $\frac{4}{5}$ of a pizza. How much pizza is eaten?

5 Four children each eat $\frac{2}{3}$ of a quiche. How much quiche is eaten?

6 Two children each eat $\frac{5}{6}$ of a cheesecake.
How much cheesecake is eaten?

7 Five children each eat $\frac{3}{4}$ of an apple pie. How much pie is eaten?

 Write a multiplication of a fraction with an answer less than 1, and a multiplication of a fraction with an answer of more than 1. They must not be on this page already!

I am confident with multiplying and converting fractions.

Work out how much of each item the monsters eat.

1. The three monsters each eat $\frac{3}{4}$ of a pizza.
   How much pizza do they eat altogether?

2. The three monsters each eat $\frac{2}{3}$ of a cake.
   How much cake do they eat altogether?

3. The three monsters each eat $\frac{2}{5}$ of a pie.
   How much pie do they eat altogether?

Copy and complete these multiplications.

4. $2 \times \frac{4}{5} = \square$

5. $9 \times \frac{2}{3} = \square$

6. $7 \times \frac{3}{4} = \square$

7. $4 \times \frac{3}{8} = \square$

8. $12 \times \frac{3}{4} = \square$

9. $15 \times \frac{2}{3} = \square$

10. $6 \times \frac{2}{5} = \square$

11. $3 \times \frac{2}{7} = \square$

THINK Is $\frac{2}{3}$ of 12 the same as $24 \times \frac{1}{3}$? Estimate first, giving a reason. Then test out your estimate.

I am confident with multiplying and converting fractions.

Write < or > between each pair of multiplications.

1   $7 \times \frac{2}{3}$ ☐ $4 \times \frac{5}{6}$

2   $6 \times \frac{3}{4}$ ☐ $7 \times \frac{3}{8}$

3   $3 \times \frac{7}{10}$ ☐ $4 \times \frac{3}{5}$

4   $4 \times \frac{5}{6}$ ☐ $4 \times \frac{5}{12}$

5   $5 \times \frac{7}{9}$ ☐ $8 \times \frac{2}{3}$

6   $15 \times \frac{1}{2}$ ☐ $10 \times \frac{5}{6}$

 Is $\frac{2}{5}$ of 15 the same as $30 \times \frac{1}{5}$? Estimate first, giving a reason. Then test out your estimate.

I am confident with multiplying and converting fractions.

Dividing fractions by whole numbers

Solve these divisions.

1 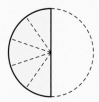 $\frac{1}{2} \div 3 = \square$

2 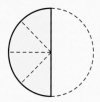 $\frac{1}{2} \div 4 = \square$

3 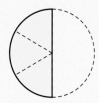 $\frac{1}{2} \div 5 = \square$

4  $\frac{1}{3} \div 2 = \square$

5 $\frac{1}{3} \div 3 = \square$

6  $\frac{1}{3} \div 4 = \square$

7 $\frac{1}{4} \div 2 = \square$

8 $\frac{1}{4} \div 3 = \square$

9  $\frac{1}{4} \div 5 = \square$

10 $\frac{1}{5} \div 2 = \square$

11 $\frac{1}{5} \div 3 = \square$

12  $\frac{1}{5} \div 4 = \square$

THINK   Draw a cake to show $\frac{1}{2} \div 6$.

○ **I am confident with dividing fractions by whole numbers.**
○
○

Solve these problems.

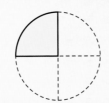

$$\frac{1}{4} \div 3 = \frac{1}{12}$$

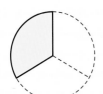

1 $\frac{1}{3} \div 5 = \square$

2 $\frac{1}{3} \div 2 = \square$

3 $\frac{1}{3} \div 4 = \square$

4 $\frac{1}{3} \div 3 = \square$

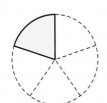

5 $\frac{1}{4} \div 4 = \square$

6 $\frac{1}{4} \div 2 = \square$

7 $\frac{1}{4} \div 5 = \square$

8 $\frac{1}{4} \div 10 = \square$

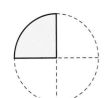

9 $\frac{1}{5} \div 3 = \square$

10 $\frac{1}{5} \div 4 = \square$

11 $\frac{1}{5} \div 5 = \square$

12 $\frac{1}{5} \div 10 = \square$

THINK Complete the calculation below giving possible values for the missing numbers. Find the four possible calculations.

$$\frac{1}{\square} \div \square = \frac{1}{18}$$

97

Solve these divisions.

1 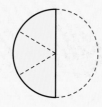 $\frac{1}{2} \div 3 = \square$

6 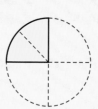 $\frac{1}{4} \div 2 = \square$

2 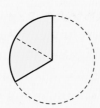 $\frac{1}{3} \div 2 = \square$

7 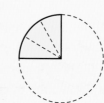 $\frac{1}{5} \div 2 = \square$

3 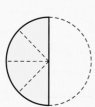 $\frac{1}{2} \div 4 = \square$

8  $\frac{1}{4} \div 3 = \square$

4  $\frac{1}{3} \div 3 = \square$

9  $\frac{1}{4} \div 4 = \square$

5 $\frac{1}{2} \div 5 = \square$

10 $\frac{1}{4} \div 5 = \square$

THINK Draw a cake to show $\frac{1}{2} \div 6$. What fraction do you get if you double your answer?

I am confident with dividing unit fractions by whole numbers.

Multiplying and dividing fractions

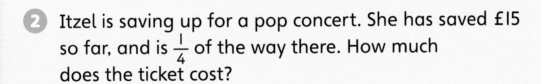

Answer these word problems.

1. Harry has 40 toy tractors in his collection. He gives $\frac{1}{5}$ of his collection to his best friend Mike. How many tractors does Mike get?

2. Itzel is saving up for a pop concert. She has saved £15 so far, and is $\frac{1}{4}$ of the way there. How much does the ticket cost?

3. Alicia ate $\frac{1}{2}$ a pancake. Tom ate a quarter of a pancake. How much did they eat altogether?

4. David, Zac and Beth were eating curry. They all ate $\frac{2}{3}$ of a poppadom each. How many poppadoms did they eat altogether?

5. After a party, there are four bottles of pop left. Each one contains $\frac{1}{3}$ of pop. How much pop is there altogether?

6. Abdul has $\frac{2}{3}$ of a pizza. He shares it equally with Lucy. How much pizza do they have each?

 **THINK** Make up a word problem for the calculation $\frac{3}{4} \times 4$.

I am confident with dividing unit fractions by whole numbers.

Answer these word problems.

1 Farmer David has 24 chickens. He gives a quarter of the chickens to Sally and a sixth of the chickens to Patience. How many chickens does he have left?

2 Poppy gives one half of a cake to her big brother and the other half to her three friends who share it equally. What fraction of the cake does each friend get?

3 Beth has done two calculations. Her teacher says one is right and one is wrong. Which one is wrong? Show Beth the correct answer.

$$\frac{1}{4} \times 3 = \frac{1}{12}$$

$$\frac{1}{8} \times 3 = \frac{3}{8}$$

4 Abshly has one-quarter of a bag of crisps. He gives the bag to three friends who share it equally. What fraction of the bag do they each have?

5 Jerry has saved £36·60. He gives a quarter of his savings to his best friend. How much does he now have?

6 Mali has half of the cost of a day trip to a theme park for two people, and Sarah has one-third of the cost. What fraction of the cost do they have?

7 Sam has one-quarter of a bar of chocolate and Zoe has one-third. What fraction of a whole bar do they have altogether?

8 Two-thirds of a pizza is left in the fridge. The cat manages to steal one-quarter of this. What fraction of the whole pizza did the cat steal?

○
○   **I am confident with multiplying and dividing fractions.**
○

1. There are 21 slices in a loaf of bread. Two-sevenths are used to make cheese sandwiches. Three-sevenths are used to make ham sandwiches. How many slices of bread are used?

2. Class 2E was asked to vote for their favourite hobby. Two-thirds of the class voted for swimming. One-quarter voted for football. The rest voted for computer games. What fraction of the class voted for a sport?

3. Three-quarters of a cheesecake was left. Alex ate one-eighth of the whole cheesecake. How much is now left?

4. Hannah had three boxes of chocolates for Christmas. She ate one-quarter of a box each day for seven days. How many boxes has she eaten? How many are left?

5. Theo has two-thirds of a box of chocolates left. He and his two sisters share the chocolates equally. What fraction of the whole box does each of them have? If the box had 54 chocolates, how many chocolates does each person eat?

6. Two brothers share three-quarters of a pie. What fraction do they get each?

 Make up a word problem for the calculation $\frac{1}{3} \div 4$.

Practising calculations

Solve these calculations.

① 985 613 − ☐ = 905 613

② 972 816 + 3023 = ☐

③ 7095 + 801 = ☐

④ 80 + 30 + 60 + 90 = ☐

⑤
$$\begin{array}{r} 7{\cdot}61 \\ 1{\cdot}92 \\ + \quad 1{\cdot}35 \\ \hline \end{array}$$

⑥ 7 × 3 + 2 = ☐

⑦ 3·69 + 6·2 = ☐

⑧ (9 − 3) × 2 = ☐

⑨ 85·66 − 30·3 = ☐

⑩ (14 − 7) × 7 + 4 = ☐

⑪ $\frac{1}{2} - \frac{1}{3}$ = ☐

⑫ 600 ÷ 25 = ☐

⑬ $\frac{1}{2} - \frac{1}{4}$ = ☐

⑭ 9 × $\frac{2}{3}$ = ☐

⑮ 7 × $\frac{3}{4}$ = ☐

⑯ 2727 ÷ 4 = ☐

⑰ 15% of £80 = ☐

⑱ (12 − 10) ÷ 2 = ☐

⑲ 81 + 76 + 23 = ☐

⑳ (3 + $\frac{1}{2}$) × 2 = ☐

㉑ 15 000 + 43 000 = ☐

㉒
$$\begin{array}{r} 4{\cdot}78 \\ 2{\cdot}47 \\ + \quad 1{\cdot}79 \\ \hline \end{array}$$

㉓ 12 ÷ (2 + 4) × 3 = ☐

㉔ 58·25 + 19·78 = ☐

㉕ 11·27 − 4·99 = ☐

㉖ 3·4 − 2·8 = ☐

㉗ 54·72 − 8·99 = ☐

㉘ 616 ÷ 8 = ☐

㉙ 5785 ÷ 7 = ☐

㉚ $\frac{1}{2} - \frac{1}{6}$ = ☐

㉛ 15 × $\frac{2}{3}$ = ☐

㉜ 6 × $\frac{2}{5}$ = ☐

㉝ 7253 ÷ 6 = ☐

㉞ 90% of £11 = ☐

If both equations are true, find the values of the letters.

㉟ 11 − m − n = 7 　　　　m × n = 4

㊱ 36 ÷ x = 3y 　　　　x + y = 8

Fraction puzzles

1 Arrange the digits 1 to 4 in the blue boxes to make a fraction addition with a mixed number answer. If all the fractions are proper fractions (not top-heavy), how many different solutions can you find?

$$\frac{\square}{\square} + \frac{\square}{\square} = \square\frac{\square}{\square}$$

2 How many more solutions can you find if you allow top-heavy fractions (still using only the digits 1 to 4)?

3 Using any digits from 1 to 9, make the statement true by filling in a different digit into each of the boxes (blue and yellow) so that no two digits are the same.

This is a fraction multiplication with a mixed number answer.

$$\frac{\square}{\square} \times \square = \square\frac{\square}{\square}$$

4 Choose three different digits to go in the blue boxes to make a multiplication with a mixed number answer.

5 Try this several times. What must you remember about the blue digits to make your answer a mixed number?

6 Look at your answers (the yellow boxes). Are any of the yellow digits of the answer the same as the blue digits in the question? If so, why is this?

7 Is it possible for none of the yellow digits to be the same as any of the blue digits? Give some examples.

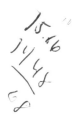

Series Editor
Ruth Merttens

Author Team
Jennie Kerwin and Hilda Merttens

Published by Pearson Education Limited, Edinburgh Gate, Harlow, Essex, CM20 2JE.

www.pearsonschools.co.uk

Text © Pearson Education Limited 2014
Page design and layout by room9design
Original illustrations © Pearson Education Limited 2014
Illustrated by Andrew Painter pp19–21, 31–35, 38–39, 47–48, 50–53, 58, 77–78, 87, 89,
91, 94, 99–101; Matt Buckley pp9–11, 18, 28, 36, 39, 42, 44, 46, 59, 68–76, 93, 96–98
Cover design by Pearson Education Limited
Cover illustration and Abacus character artwork by Volker Beisler © Pearson Education Limited
Additional contributions by Hilary Koll and Steve Mills, CME Projects Ltd.
First published 2014

16
10 9 8 7 6 5 4

British Library Cataloguing in Publication Data
A catalogue record for this book is available from the British Library

ISBN 978 1 408 27856 7

Printed in Slovakia

Acknowledgements
We would like to thank the staff and pupils at North Kidlington Primary School, Haydon Wick Primary School, Swindon, St Mary's Catholic Primary School, Bodmin, St Andrew's C of E Primary & Nursery School, Sutton-in-Ashfield, Saint James' C of E Primary School, Southampton and Harborne Primary School, Birmingham, for their invaluable help in the development and trialling of this book.

Every effort has been made to contact copyright holders of material reproduced in this book. Any omissions will be rectified in subsequent printings if notice is given to the publishers.